Bridge-Logos
Alachua, FL 32615 USA

2012: Is This the End?
by Lloyd Hildebrand

Library of Congress Catalog Card Number: 2009928132
International Standard Book Number 978-0-88270-965-9

Unless otherwise indicated, Scripture quotations in this book are from the *King James Version* of the Bible.

Scripture quotations marked NIV are taken from the *Holy Bible, New International Version*®. NIV®. Copyright © 1973, 1978, 1984 by International Bible Society. Used by permission of Zondervan. All rights reserved.

G163.316.N.m905.35260

DEDICATION

To my lovely, supportive, and always faithful wife, Peggy;

My strong and handsome sons:
Paul, David, Mark, Tim, and Jeff;

My beautiful daughters-in-law:
Carie, Jessica, Christie, and Nicki;

My talented and happy grandchildren:
Zoe, Max, Noah, Sam, Jack, Thomas, Hunter,
Alicia, Breeona, Cecilia, Dessie, Eden, Gianna, Nathan,
Taylor, and Tim.

I love you all very much.
Thank you for being such a special family.

CONTENTS

INTRODUCTION

This book will challenge you, inspire you, fascinate you, and cause you to think about the end of the world and the future of humanity.

What is going to happen on December 21, 2012? Will the world come to an end on that day—the winter solstice of 2012—as many ancient and more recent prophecies predict?

So many seers, prophets, and calendars point to this date as being either the end of the world as we know it or the dawning of a new age and a new world. Are there any reasons for us to believe these prognostications?

This book takes a close look at the prophecies related to December 21, 2012, and other end-time prophecies, in an effort to find answers to the following questions:

- Will the world come to an end? Is it possible to know when?
- What does the Bible say about the end times?
- Are we living in the last days?
- From what sources may prophecies be derived?
- Is there any evidence to back up these prophecies?
- What should we believe about the future?
- Is there any hope for mankind?
- What role will the anti-Christ play? Is it possible to know who he is?
- Will earthquakes, wars, famines, tsunamis, terrorism, global climate changes, and other phenomena increase in both frequency and intensity?

- How did people in ancient times differ from people today?
- How can we best prepare for the end?

We will take a careful look at each of these questions as we read about the eschatological predictions that were given by the Mayans, the Q'ero Incas, the Toltecs, the Aztecs, the Cherokees, the Hopis, the Chinese, the Hindus, Merlin the Magician, Nostradamus, Mother Shipton, Buddhists, Zoroastrians, Hebrews, Muslims, the holy Bible, and various other sources.

We will also examine certain scientific theories about the future and what could happen to our planet and our people.

During these perilous times of international economic recession, high unemployment rates, tensions between nations, mortgage foreclosures, suicides, bankruptcies, natural disasters, terrorism, fear, and uncertainty, finding satisfactory answers to questions about the future is important and vital to each of us. My hope and prayer is that this book will help you in your search for truth, peace, and spiritual understanding regarding the future.

In addition to the circumstances I've cited above, basic morality and integrity appear to be on the decline. This reality adds to our concern about the future. Please note that I use the word *concern* instead of the word *fear.* As you read this book, let truth and wisdom overcome all worry and fear you may have with regard to future events. There are answers to many of the questions I present in this book, and those answers will help to lift us above the circumstances of life and any prophecies of gloom and doom.

Let us take a serious look at what has happened, what is happening, and what might happen in an effort to get ready for the future. By the time you finish your reading of this book, you will see that God has a plan for your life—a plan for a good future, even though we may well be living in the last days.

If the fulfillment of certain prophetic events is imminent, as many cultures and religions believe, it is crucial for you to get prepared, at least spiritually, for everything that may lie ahead. In this book you will learn how to do so, and this will give you peace of heart, a sense of security, and a serene outlook.

So, read this book with an open mind. I'm sure its findings will intrigue you, trouble you, surprise you, arouse your curiosity, and enlighten you. The concluding chapter will even inspire you and motivate you to take positive action during these challenging times.

2012: Is This the End? attempts to gather available research and to present the variety of theories and speculations about the end times in an objective manner, so that you can draw your own conclusions about these matters. Toward the end of the book I share my own personal views regarding eschatology (the study of the end times). As you will see, my conclusions are based on extensive study, prayer, analysis, contemplation, and research.

As you begin to read, keep these words of Dorothy Thompson in mind: "Only when we are no longer afraid do we begin to live."

Do you fear the future?

1

THE MAYAN LONG-COUNT CALENDAR AND THE PROPHECIES OF PACAL VOTAN

... on December 20, 2012, Mother Earth will pass inside the center of a magnetic axis and ... it may be darkened with a great cloud for 60 to 70 hours and that because of environmental degradation, she may not be strong enough to survive the effects. It will enter another age, but when it does, there will be great and serious events. Earthquakes, marementos [tsunamis], floods, volcanic eruptions and great illness on the planet Earth. Few survivors will be left.
DON ALEJANDRO, MAYAN ELDER

William Faulkner wrote, "Clocks slay time ... time is dead as long as it is being clicked off by little wheels; only when the clock stops does time come to life."

When will the clock stop? The Mayans had something to say about this and many other related topics. We can't ignore their prophecies. These people spent a great deal of time observing nature and its cycles, and they have something important to say to us today.

What is your relationship with time? Is it your master, or your servant? In this chapter you will learn about the Mayan view of time, and you will understand why they seemed to believe that history would end on December 21, 2012.

As you will see, this is a very significant date, indeed.

CHICHEN ITZA PYRAMID

WHO WERE THE MAYANS?

The Mayan culture developed a relatively complex civilization in the present-day regions of Mexico and Central America (Guatemala, Belize, El Salvador, and Honduras). The Yucatan Peninsula (in eastern Mexico) probably was the site of their earliest settlements in approximately 2600 BC.

The Mayan civilization lasted for many centuries (from 2600 BC to AD 1500) and was perhaps the best known of all the classical cultures of Mesoamerica. It rose to prominence during the Classical Era (approximately AD 250 to AD 900). The Mayan civilization was very highly advanced. They had their own writing system (a logosyllabic system), which has enabled us to understand them better, and they placed great emphasis upon astronomy (astrology), mathematics, and architecture. Their well-constructed buildings—temples, pyramids, palaces, and observatories—have stood the test of time, and it is amazing to realize that these structures were built without the use of metal tools or any form of modern technology.

One wonders how these ancient people acquired such advanced knowledge, and many have speculated that it may have come from extraterrestrial sources.

Tourists who travel to Cancun and other parts of Mexico find visits to Mayan ruins, such as Tulum and Chichen Itza, to be very fascinating and enlightening. Upon visiting such sites, the traveler is immediately impressed with Mayan skills in architecture and astronomy.

The artwork of this Mesoamerican culture is colorful, unique, and beautiful. In fact, the Mayans were true masters in the visual arts, weaving, and pottery.

Mayan people felt very close to nature, and their economy was based on a maize-centered agriculture. Maize was an extremely important food to them, and one of their deities watched over its cultivation.

Oftentimes, modern people tend to look condescendingly upon people who lived in ancient times. Frequently, these earlier people are referred to as "primitive cultures." However, when we examine the lives and mores of these people more closely, we discover that they may have been more advanced than we are in many ways.

For one thing, their spiritual values had great priority in their lives. They felt very close to nature and learned a great deal from observing natural cycles and systems. Though their approaches to knowledge and understanding may have differed greatly from our own, it is clear that they arrived at a measure of truth and endeavored to walk in wisdom.

What can we learn from the Mayans and their folkways? What do they have to say to modern man?

THE MAYAN CALENDARS

The Mayans put great emphasis upon the cycles of nature, and we see this in the calendars they developed, which were intricate and precise. Their long-count calendar was quite different from the calendars we use today.

They based the development of their calendars on their astronomical observations. The Mayan preoccupation with time resulted in the development of an extremely accurate and precise calendar—a calendar that was able to predict solar eclipses with great accuracy thousands of years in advance.

Most of the modern world follows the Gregorian calendar, which was established by Pope Gregory XIII in 1582. The calendars of the Mayan culture are very different from the Gregorian calendar, as you will see in the following paragraphs.

The Mayan calendars do much more than simply track the passage of time. Instead, they are designed to describe the progression of the heavens and the underworld (the realm of the dead), to help us understand the past, to put forth prophecies about the future, and to provide an exact schedule for the overall cosmic plan.

Unlike people today, the Mayans did not view time as a quantity; rather, they saw it as being a quality, and they regarded their calendars as being open doors to the fourth dimension—the spiritual realm. The Mayans encouraged people to use these calendars in such a way that they would be lifted out of the physical realm, including basic concepts of space and time.

They emphasized the importance of practicing the present moment. There is much we can learn from their perspective regarding time.

According to the Mayans, there is precise order to the universe and everything happens for specific reasons. Their calendars represented the universe itself—a wheel of time in which everything is interconnected.

The Mayans believed in the existence of a dark rift in the center of the Milky Way, and scientists have recently confirmed that this "dark rift" actually does exist.

The Winter Solstice of 2012

This brings us to the central focus of this book—*December 21, 2012.* What does the Mayan long-count calendar have to say about this date, and on what is this conclusion based?

December 21, 2012, is the final day of the Mayan calendar—the end of time and possibly the end of the world. The Mayans regard this day as the point when human history could come to a close.

The period immediately prior to that date has also been called: "The Time of Trial on Earth," "Judgment Day," "The Time of Great Purification," "The End of This Creation," "The Quickening," "The End of Time as We Know It," and "The Shift of the Ages."[1]

5

THE MILKY WAY

It is clear that the Mayans (and several other cultures and individuals) regard December 21, 2012, as a day when tumultuous and climactic changes will take place. This belief stems from the Mayan concept of cycles and one of those cycles in particular—"The Precession of the Equinoxes"—which involves a 26,000-year period in which the Earth transits through each of the twelve signs of the Zodiac.[2]

Even though the Mayan and Hindu cultures presumably had no contact with each other, it is interesting to note that ancient Hindu mythology concurs with Mayan thoughts about the emergence of a new world (the "Golden Age") around 2012. The ancient Hindus used both lunar and solar calendars to make their predictions.

The Hindu Kali Yuga calendar began on February 18, 3102 BC. This is approximately when the Mayan's Fifth Great Cycle began, as well. Amazingly, both the Mayan and Hindu calendars started at about the same time and both calendars predict a totally new world emerging around 2012.[3]

The Mayans saw the 26,000-year period I mentioned above as being divided into five cycles, and each of these cycles was believed to be approximately 5,125 years long; each was also considered to be its own "world age" or "creation cycle." The Aztec Calendar (the sun stone), which we will discuss more fully in a later chapter, shows each of these cycles as being ruled and destroyed by one of the five natural elements.

The following chart shows the various divisions related to the long-count calendar:

1. The Precession of the Equinoxes—26,000 years. This period is known as the Grand Cosmic Year.

2. The Five Creation Cycles—5,125 years each. (The Fifth Great Cycle began in 3114 BC, and it will end on December 21, 2012.)

3. Baktuns—Cycles of 394 years (or 144,000 days) each.

4. The Transition Through the Twelve Signs of the Zodiac—Each era lasts approximately 2,152 Years.

THE END OF HISTORY

According to the Mayans, we are currently in the Age of the Fifth Sun, which involves the synthesis of the previous four cycles. In his book, *Time and the Technosphere*, Dr. Jose Arguelles writes, "August 13, 3113 BC is as precise and accurate as one can get for the beginning of history: the first Egyptian dynasty is dated to 3100 BC; the first 'city,' Uruk, in Mesopotamia, also ca 3100 BC; the Hindu Kali Yuga, 3102 BC; and most interestingly, the division of time into 24 hours of 60 minutes each and each minute into 60 seconds [and the division of the circle into 360 degrees], also around 3100 BC, in Sumeria. If the beginning of history was accurately placed, then must not the end of history, December 21, 2012, also be as accurate?"[4]

The Mayans believed that knowing the past meant knowing the cyclical influences that work together to create the present and the future. They (and the Aztecs, as well as others) believed that the world had been created and destroyed five times. According to them, the Fifth Great Cycle began in 3114 BC, and it will end on December 21, 2012.

The Mayans believed that as the final day approaches, mankind will give in to materialism, and matter will be transformed. The final *baktun*—our present age—was prophesied to be a time of great forgetting, a time when mankind would drift far away from any sense of oneness with nature.

Were they right about this? Has modern man lost his relationship with nature? Have people become greedy and materialistic?

The Mayan long-count calendar further reveals that on December 21, 2012, there will be an extremely close conjunction of the winter-solstice sun with the crossing point of the Galactic Equator (Equator of the Milky Way) and the Ecliptic Path of the Sun. When this happens, the Mayans believe that their "sacred tree"—a veritable cross—will appear in the heavens.

Science tends to agree with this prediction. When the winter solstice of 2012 arrives on December 21, the sun will be aligned with the center of the Milky Way for the first time in approximately 26,000 years (the Grand Cosmic Year, as defined by the Mayans). About this near-future celestial event, Lawrence Joseph writes, "... whatever energy typically streams to Earth from the center of the Milky Way will be disrupted on 12/21/12 at 11:11 PM Universal Time."[5]

Science has no way of knowing what effect this will have upon our planet, but the Mayans seemed to believe the results will be catastrophic. There is a black hole in the center of our galaxy. In 2012, the sun and the Earth will be in direct alignment with this black hole. This may cause magnetic shifts to take place, and might even result in the shifting of the poles. It is believed that the poles have shifted before, and in 1955, Albert Einstein postulated that such a polar shift might occur.[6]

One thing is certain. The Mayans were right about modern civilization's turn away from nature and our high materialistic values. Jesus said, *"No man can serve two masters: for either he will hate the one, and love the other; or else he will hold to the one, and despise the other. Ye cannot serve God and mammon"* (Matthew 6:24).

WHO WAS PACAL VOTAN?

Pacal Votan (aka K'inich Janaab' Pakal) was the ruler of the Mayan Empire of Nah Chan Palenque. He was also known as Pacal the Great.

Votan lived from AD 603 to AD 683. (This was during the period when the Mayans became very prominent.) He ascended to the throne when he was only twelve, and ruled for almost seventy years.

Lid of the Sarcophagus of Pacal Votan

When he died in 683, his body was placed in the Temple of Inscriptions in Palenque. His final resting place was a sarcophagus that was lavishly decorated with his own image and various symbols representing the sun, the moon, and several constellations. Underneath him is a portrayal of the Mayan god of the underworld.

Was Votan an Ancient Astronaut?

In his famous book, *Chariots of the Gods*, Erich von Daniken suggests that Votan was actually an astronaut. He perceived that some of the glyphs on the lid of the sarcophagus depict rockets and other space-travel equipment and paraphernalia. In saying this, von Daniken is expressing his belief that the Mayans were influenced by extraterrestrials and that their forebears may have come from outer space.

Some people believe this theory, and they are convinced that the Mayans were greatly influenced by extraterrestrial intelligence.

Here is von Daniken's description of the scenes that are portrayed on the coffin lid: "In the center of that frame is a man [Votan] sitting, bending forward. He has a mask on his nose, he uses his two hands to manipulate some controls, and the heel of his left foot is on a kind of pedal with different adjustments. The rear portion is separated from him; he is sitting on a complicated chair, and outside of this whole frame, you see a little flame like an exhaust."(From *Chariots of the Gods* by Erich von Daniken.)

What do you think? This is certainly an interesting and highly imaginative theory, but it is a very dubious one at best. One Mayanist, Ian Graham, reacted to von Daniken's theory as follows: "Well, I certainly don't see a need to regard him as a space man. I don't see any oxygen tubes. I see a very characteristically drawn Maya face."

Whatever the case, Votan was highly regarded by his people as an enlightened soul, a man whom they believed possessed the wisdom of the gods.[8]

ANCIENT ASTRONAUT THEORIES

Has the Earth been visited by extraterrestrial beings? Have these entities helped to develop ancient cultures all over the world? Some have suggested that the gods of ancient religions were actually visitors from outer space.

Erich von Daniken and Zechariah Sitchin are two notable proponents of the Ancient Astronaut Theory. These men and several others have looked at some of the artifacts and remains of ancient civilizations, particularly those that seem to be more advanced than would have been expected in an earlier era, and have concluded that these things were made possible through the teaching and direction of extraterrestrials. These "ancient astronauts" are seen as having been the "mother culture" to the ancients, such as the Mayans, the Druids, the Egyptians, and many others.

Some of the artwork of earlier cultures, according to these researchers, appears to depict extraterrestrial beings, as well. Notable scientists, such as Carl Sagan, I.S. Shklovskii, and

Hermann Oberth, have given serious consideration to this theory, as well.[9]

The advocates of the Ancient Astronaut Theory cite the following as examples of specific evidence to back up this theory:

• Certain artifacts and structures, such as the megaliths of Stonehenge, the statues on Easter Island, the Antikythera Mechanism (a 2,000-year-old clock-like mechanism), and the ancient Baghdad electric batteries (batteries from Babylonia that could actually conduct electricity).

• Certain depictions in ancient art and icons seem to show air and space vehicles. These include the lid of Votan's sarcophagus and several other works of art.

• Many ancient religious writings could be interpreted as referring to extraterrestrials. Some believe the Nephilim, giants that are mentioned in the Book of Genesis, other Scriptures, and non-canonical Jewish writings, may have been extraterrestrial aliens. Another biblical example of this speculation about visitors from outer space is found in the Book of Ezekiel. (See Ezekiel chapter one. In this passage the Prophet Ezekiel writes about a wheel-like vehicle coming from the heavens. He describes "the passengers" within the wheel in very vivid terms.)

• Ancient mythology is another source of evidence that is relied upon by these theorists. For example, "flying machines" are often depicted in ancient texts. (A good example of this is found in the Sanskrit epics of India, which discuss the Vimanas—flying machines.)

• Ancient "model airplanes" have been discovered in Egypt and South America. (Some believe these resemble modern airplanes and gliders; others believe they are simply representing certain birds.)

• Some Medieval and Renaissance art shows entities that could be interpreted to be flying saucers. (Certain theorists believe this shows that the extraterrestrial creators of mankind return to check up on their creation from time to time.)

• Paleolithic cave paintings. Some of these paintings, particularly the *Vondijina* in Australia and the Val Camonica in Italy, seem to resemble modern-day astronauts.

• *Nazca Lines.* The Nazca Lines of Peru are a large group of huge drawings that are found on the ground. These drawings can only be viewed from the air. Some believe that these drawings were developed in order to communicate with extraterrestrials.

• Ancient monuments and megaliths. The pyramids of Egypt, Machu Picchu in Peru, and Baalbek in Lebanon were erected or constructed without modern technology and appear to go beyond the technological abilities of people in those eras.

These theories are fascinating, to be sure, and science fiction has built many a novel upon the foundation provided by these speculations. Has the Earth been visited by beings from outer space? If so, are these beings physical or spiritual in nature? If these entities exist, are they friendly? These three questions remain unanswered, though there is much speculation surrounding each of them.

THE TELEKTONON

Found within Pacal Votan's tomb was an "Earth-speaking tube," which is also known as a telektonon. His followers believed that the departed emperor was able to communicate with them from the afterlife through this tube.[10]

Lord Pacal Votan taught his disciples about many things. For example, he told them about a past civilization whose ruins are beneath the sea. (Could this be the famed Atlantis?)

Without doubt, his people believed Votan was an extraordinary seer and magician who possessed supernatural powers and divine knowledge. It is interesting to note that he

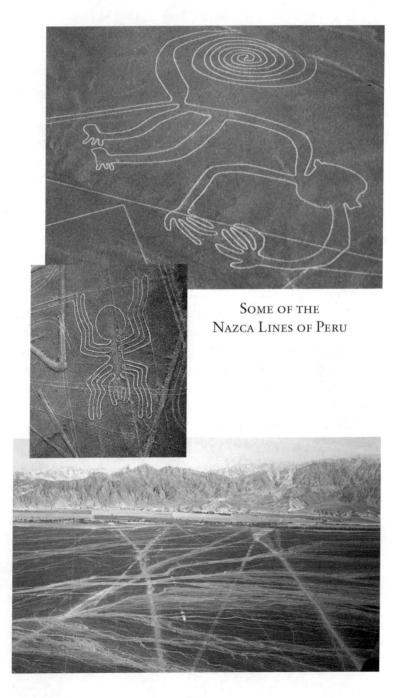

Some of the
Nazca Lines of Peru

taught about a form of meditation that is based on chakras that are similar to those of Kundalini Hinduism. He told the Mayans that these chakras were sources of great power that could be employed by those who learn how to activate them.

This was a form of esoteric knowledge that Votan surmised could only be gained through spiritual enlightenment.

A Transition of Consciousness

Votan referred to a future "transition of consciousness," which would occur prior to and close to December 21, 2012. He said that this would be the closing of a world-age cycle. He prophesied that this transition phase would represent the death of the old world and the beginning of a new world.

This highly respected emperor predicted that the time would come when human beings would leave the things of nature and give themselves over to the pursuit of material things. He warned that this would cause us to lose sight of our interdependence with nature and that mankind, as a result, would never get back into harmony with the timing of the natural universe.

Votan was a mathematician, as well. He regarded mathematics as a higher type of language that transcends the subjectivity of human verbal experience. He said, "All is number. God is a number. God is in all."[11]

Some have called Pacal Votan "Time's Special Witness." He proclaimed, "If humanity wishes to save itself from biospheric destruction, it must return to living in natural time."[12]

By the phrase, "living in natural time" Votan was referring to a transition of consciousness. This involves so much more than simply tracking the passage of time.

In fact, the Mayan view of time is something we need to consider in the present day. Are we preoccupied with concerns about the past or the future? How can we learn to practice the present moment more fully? Have the values of materialism caused us to lose sight of the beauty, importance, and wisdom that are to be found within nature?

Does guilt over the past and a fear of the future prevent you from living fully in the present moments of your life? Have you learned to live in the now of your life?

As you can see, we make a serious mistake when we look upon earlier cultures as being inferior to our own simply because their knowledge of science and other subjects was different from ours. Though the Mayans' view of time differs substantially from ours, does this mean they were wrong?

Their view of time was their perception of truth and, therefore, it was their reality. What can we learn from their point of view? Are there understandings and applications we can take from their spiritual perspective, as well?

What if they were right about the end of time?

Is December 21, 2012, the final day of life on Earth?

"Live this day as if it will be your last. Remember that you will only find 'tomorrow' on the calendars of fools. Forget yesterday's defeats and ignore the problems of tomorrow. This is it. Doomsday. All you have. Make it the best day of your year" (Og Mandino).

ENDNOTES

1. *The Living Prophecy*. http://www.13moon.com/
prophecy%20page.htm

2. Ibid.

3. *Hindu Mayan Connection*. http://wikibin.org/articles/hindu-mayan-connection.html

4. *The Living Prophecy*. http://www.13moon.com/
prophecy%20page.htm

5. Joseph, Lawrence. *Apocalypse 2012*, 2007. Broadway Books.

6. Peterson, Carl, *Polar Shift by 2012? New Evidence and Theory Suggests Einstein May Have Been Right*. http://EzineArticles.com/?expert=Carl_Peterson

7. *Pacal the Great*. http://en.wikipedia.org/wiki/Pacal_the-Great

8. Ibid.

9. *Ancient Astronaut Theory*. http://2012wiki.com/index.php?title=Ancient_astronaut-theory

10. *Time's Special Witness*. www.holisticwebs.com/earthwizard/index9.html

11. *Pacal Votan Sage-King of the Classic Maya*. www.13moon.com/pacal%20link.htm

12. *The Living Prophecy*. http://www.13moon.com/
prophecy%20page.htm

**Other Resources That Were Consulted in the
Preparation of This Chapter Include**

1. *The Mayan Prophecies for 2012* by Gerald Benedict. Published by Watkins Publishing, London, in 2008.

2. http://www.usatoday.com/tech/scienc/2007-03-27-maya-2012_n.htm

3. http://www.december212012.com/articles/news/Many_gather_to_ponder_end_of _Maya

4. http://www.december212012.com/articles/news/Thousands_Expect_Apocalypse_in_2012

5. http://www.greatdreams.com/2012.htm

6. http://www.experiencefestival.com/mayan_calendar
7. http://2012-predictions-review.blogspot.com/2008/05/pacal-votan.html
8. http://www.digitalmeesh.com/maya/history.htm
9. http://en.wikipedia.org/wiki/Maya_civilization

Additional Resources You May Wish to Explore

1. *The Lost Chronicles of the Maya Kings* by David Drew. Published by Phoenix Press, London, 2004.
2. *The Gods and Symbols of Ancient Mexico and the Maya* by Mary Miller and Karl Taube. Published by Thames & Hudson, London, 1993.
3. *The Fall of the Ancient Maya* by David L. Webster. Published by Thames & Hudson, London, 2002.
4. *Maya History and Religion* by J. Eric S. Thompson. Published by University of Oklahoma Press, 1970.s

2

THE PROPHECIES OF THE Q'ERO INCA SHAMANS

*The new caretakers of the Earth will come from the West,
and those that have made the greatest impact on Mother
Earth now have the moral responsibility to remake their
relationship with her, after remaking themselves.*
DON ANTONIO MORALES, Q'ERO SHAMAN[1]

It would appear that Morales (in the quote above) is referring to the Europeans who settled in the New World. Certainly their impact upon "Mother Earth" has been profound, and a great portion of that impact has been very harmful. Air and water pollution, the use of nuclear weapons, chemical contaminations of various sorts, strip mining and other methods of mining, and many other forms of devastation have been commonplace in recent decades.

Are we exercising our moral responsibility with regard to nature? Have we been good stewards of the Earth and its natural resources? Have we begun remaking our relationship to nature? Are we learning to remake ourselves? These are certainly crucial questions to consider in this present age, and in this chapter we will take a good look at each of them.

As you will see, there are many commonalities between the Mayans and the Q'ero Incas. The importance of nature and the value of time are two of these.

LAKE TITICACA

A Swiss physician and alchemist of the Renaissance, Paracelsus, wrote, "Time is a brisk wind, for each hour it brings something new ... but who can understand and measure its sharp breath, its mystery and its design?"

The wind of time continues to blow upon our lives. Where will it take us? As you read the words of the Q'ero Inca shamans, you will gain some new insights into mankind's relationship with time.

Is there anything to be learned from these ancient Inca prophecies? As we in the Western World are today, the Incas were the prevailing culture of their region and era. What were the sources of their knowledge? How did they arrive at their conclusions? What was their view of time and the future?

Did these people know something we do not know? In this chapter you will learn about a predicted transition in the human heart that many believe has already begun to take place. This is very similar to what Pacal Votan referred to as being the transition of consciousness.

WHO ARE THE Q'ERO PEOPLE?

The Q'ero are believed to be the last of the Incas—a native culture that developed in present-day Peru. They escaped from the Spanish conquistadors by taking refuge not far from Lake Titicaca, high in the Andes Mountains. For half a millennium they have survived at elevations exceeding fourteen thousand feet. They lived in isolation on these mountaintops until they were "rediscovered" in 1949 by an anthropologist named Oscar Nunez del Prado. The first Western expedition to the Q'ero villages took place six years later.[2]

The Q'ero—a tribe of a few hundred people—live in one of the most remote places in the Andes. Their houses are made of clay and stone and are topped with grass roofs.

THE GREAT CHANGE

For the past five hundred years the Q'ero people have been the careful stewards of Inca prophecies that were recorded long ago. One of these prophecies—the *pachacuti*—predicts great changes for planet Earth that the Q'ero believe will be taking place in the very near future. In fact, they believe these changes have already begun.

The Andean shamans say, "Follow your own footsteps. Learn from the rivers, the trees and the rocks. Honor the Christ, the Buddha, your brothers and sisters. Honor the Mother Earth and the Great Spirit. Honor yourself and all creation."[3]

In the above quote we see the high regard the Q'ero give to creation. They have also endeavored to incorporate the ideas of many religions, including Christianity and Buddhism, into their belief system, and one of their highest values is love. As you will see, they give great priority to nature and its cycles, as well.

The *pachacuti* is a sacred prophecy that predicts a "great change" in which the world will be turned right-side-up, harmony and order will be restored, and chaos and disorder will be ended.

When the Spanish conquered the Incas approximately five hundred years ago, the last *pachacuti* (or great change) took place. These people believe that civilization and the Earth are now getting ready for the next great change—the final transition.

The prophecies they have given are relatively optimistic. Though the Q'ero do believe in the end of the age, they see this climax as being the end of time as we know it—the death of a way of thinking and a way of being. They foresee a time in the not-too-distant future when we will enter a golden age—a millennium of peace.

When will all this take place? The Q'ero say that the chaos and turmoil that have been so much a part of life throughout history will last until 2012! From then on, things will be very different, and the remainder of this chapter endeavors to spell out those differences with clarity and specificity.

INCAN RELIGION

The religion of the Incas is polytheistic, but their most important god is Inti—the sun. Their deities occupy three different realms:

1. The celestial realm is overseen by the god Hanan Paca.
2. The inner-earth realm is overseen by the god Ukhu Paca.
3. The outer-earth realm (where we live) is overseen by the god Cay Paca.

There are several other deities in their pantheon, as well, and each has specific and particular spheres of responsibility.

This people believes in the duality of the cosmos—a concept that is akin to Taoism and other Eastern religions.

HUMAN SACRIFICES

Like many other Mesoamerican groups, the Incas practiced ritual human sacrifices. The sacrificed ones were usually children or slaves. These sacrifices were reserved for very special occasions, such as the enthronement of a king. At such a coronation, as many as two hundred children would be killed. Human sacrifices also took place in times of famine and other crises. It was considered to be an honor to die as a sacrificial offering to the gods.

Why did tragedies, such as famines and epidemics, require a human sacrifice? It is because such calamities were regarded as punishment for disobedience and sinfulness. Such sins called for repentance, a confession of sin, and a blood sacrifice.

These are themes we find in many ancient religions, including Judaism.

According to the Incas, every person possesses two souls. After death, one soul returns to its place of origin, while the second soul remains in the body, which they endeavored to preserve intact through mummification.

In addition to the deities of their religion, the Incas worshiped the dead, their ancestors, heroes from history, and their king, who was considered to be divine. They viewed nature and its cycles as being very sacred, as well, and this led them to cherish and give high importance to both time and space.

Like the Mayans, the Incas' calendar was spiritual in nature. Each month had its own religious festival. For example, the month we call January was set aside as a time for fasting and penitence.

The Incas believed strongly in prophecy. They used divination to help them make predictions regarding the outcome of battles, social events, and supernatural occurrences. Through divination they predicted whether one's illness would be healed, determined what sacrifices should be made to their gods, and discovered who had committed certain crimes.

The Incas consulted their "oracles" by watching the movements of a spider in a dish, observing how cocoa leaves fell, and by drinking an hallucinogenic concoction known as *ayahuasca*. They would also examine the markings within the lungs of a sacrificed llama in order to attempt to peer into the future.

Prophecy was an important aspect of life in the Inca civilization, as it was in most cultures during ancient times.

INCAN PROPHECIES

The Prophecy of the Great Change that we alluded to earlier goes into some detail with regard to specific changes

THE EAGLE AND
THE CONDOR
WILL FLY AGAIN.

that have been prophesied—changes that the shamans believe will take place in the next few years. Their spiritual leaders have said that "the peoples of the four directions" will soon be reintegrated. They symbolize this by saying that the eagle of the North and the condor of the South will fly again. (This is interpreted as meaning that North and South America will soon be reunited.)

They believe that *manay* (love and compassion) will be the guiding principle behind this "great gathering." They foresee this reunification of peoples as being facilitated by North America supplying the physical strength, Europe supplying the mental prowess, and South America supplying the heart.[4]

MACHU PICCHU

These prophecies stress unity, togetherness, and co-operation among all people.

Is this a desirable goal? Is it realistic?

THE NEW MAN

According to Q'ero prophecies, a new type of human being will emerge in the very near future as a result of the tumultuous changes that will take place on Earth. These changes will definitely affect the human psyche and redefine our relationships with one another and with divinity.

They foresee the collapse of Western civilization and a return to the way of the "Earth People"—the Incas. These prophecies go so far as to say that the very fabric of time will be torn asunder during this final era, as well.

Some believe that Pachacuti, a great Incan leader who lived during the late 1300's and whose name is given to the great changes that will take place, will return in the very near future. Many believe this man was the architect behind the construction of Machu Picchu. They have called him a "luminous one," a man who they believed actually stepped outside of time.[5]

Pachacuti is also seen as a man who embodies the essence of the Incan prophecies. His name literally means, "transformer of the Earth." He has become a symbol of human promise and potential—unlimited potential—to those who believe in him.[6]

Though some believe that Pachacuti will literally return to Earth in order to defeat those who took the Incas' land, another segment sees him as representing the positive changes that are about to occur in mankind. Dr. Alberto Villoldo writes, "It's not the return of a single individual who embodies what we are becoming, but a process of emergence available to all peoples."[7]

Seeds of Knowledge

At a gathering in New York City in the autumn of 1996, a small band of Q'ero, including a shaman and a tribal leader, performed a private ceremony at the Cathedral of Saint John the Divine. It is believed that this Inca ritual had not been performed for five hundred years or so.

Through this ceremony the Q'ero intended to sow the seeds of spiritual knowledge among Westerners who were learning about them and their ways, including the Dean of the Cathedral of Saint John the Divine. This event was seen as providing a symbolic link between North and South America, as well as Christianity and the Incan religion.

The Q'ero shamans administered the *Mosoq Karpay*—a ceremony that is designed to break the individual's relationship with time and to release the energies of one's ancestors within the recipient's heart.[8]

The Q'ero view this ritual as planting the seeds of knowledge within the human heart. After this happens, the individual is responsible for watering, tending, and cultivating the seeds. This enables them to take root, to grow, to blossom, and to bear fruit.

All of this is symbolic of the transference of potential that enables the individual to fulfill his or her destiny—the fruit-bearing stage in the process.

The Rites of the Time to Come

The Q'ero take an esoteric view of their prophecies. They believe that these predictions are not of use unless an individual possesses the keys to understanding them through the rites of passage (the Star Rites, or the Rites of the Time to Come). These rites, according to the Q'ero, are essential to all spiritual understanding.

One of these rites involves the end of the individual's relationship to time. This is regarded as a transition that takes place within the human heart. It is very much a process of becoming, and this process is seen as being more important than any prophecy ever could be.

The Q'ero also believe that the "doorways" between the worlds are opening again and that we will be able to step through those portals and go beyond "the holes in time." This, according to their belief system, will lead to greater human capabilities being released in society. They also believe that those who are truly willing to "take the leap" will be able to regain the luminous nature that was intended for them.

According to Q'ero philosophy, the changes that have begun will be completed in 2012, and this will present us with an opportunity to describe ourselves not as who we have been (in the past), but as who we are now becoming (in the present and the future).

The teaching of the Q'ero is expressed well in the following quotation: "Look with the eyes of your soul and engage the essential" (Morgana's Observatory).

What is the essential? The three main points of Q'ero teaching are:

1. Leave the past behind.
2. Disregard the differences among people.
3. Change your relationship with time.

Changing our relationship with time involves forgetting the past, seizing the present moment and living it to the full, and it also involves avoiding worry about the future. This is what will happen in the end times or the last days, according to the Q'ero, who feel we must learn to step outside of time—the only way true transformation can take place.

Instead of focusing on the differences among people, the Q'ero want us to strive for unity and cooperation. As we learn to come together, good things will happen throughout the Earth. Until that happens, we will be governed by prejudice, bigotry, and even hatred.

From their point of view, each of us must come down from the mountaintop in a spiritual way, as the Q'ero have done physically. In this way we can all enter the age of "the One" (unity) in peace and mutual understanding.[9]

Talia Shafir sums up core principles of Q'ero teaching as follows: "So the 'end of times' takes on a new meaning. And the apocalyptic scenario of 'the end of days' seems to morph into an evolutionary modification of our relationship to time."[10]

What is your relationship with time? Do you see it as something that is measured by clocks and calendars, or as a living reality that gives birth to change?

Is what we call "Doomsday" a day of doom or a whole new beginning?

"One of the illusions of life is that the present hour is not the critical, decisive hour. Write it on your heart that every day is the best day in the year. No man has learned anything rightly, until he knows that every day is Doomsday" (Ralph Waldo Emerson).

Endnotes

1. *The Inca Prophecy.* http://www.labyrinthia.com/prophecy.htm
2. Ibid.
3. *Prophecies of the Q'ero Inca Shamans.* http://www.adishakti. org/_/prophecies_of_the_qero_inca_shamans.htm
4. Ibid.
5. Ibid.
6. Ibid.
7. Ibid.
8. Ibid.
9. *Keepers of the Prophecy.* http://newagetravel.com/keepers-prophecy.shtml
10. Ibid.

Other Resources That Were Consulted in the Preparation of This Chapter

1. *Incan Prophecies.* http://www.crystalinks.com /incan2.html
2. What's New? http://www.diagnosis2012.co.uk/new.htm
3. *Q'ero.* http://en.wikipedia.org/wiki/Qero
4. *Inca Religion.* http://en.wikipedia.org/wiki/Inca_religion

Additional Resources You May Wish to Explore

1. *Everyday Life of the Incas* by Ann Kendall, 1989.

3

TOLTEC, ITZA-MAYA, AND AZTEC PROPHECIES

*Take pains to make yourselves friends of God who is in all
parts, and is invisible and impalpable, and it is meet that you
give Him all your heart and body, and look that you be not
proud in your heart, nor yet despair, nor be cowardly of spirit;
but that you be humble in your heart and have hope in God.
Be at peace with all, shame yourselves before none and to
none be disrespectful; respect all, esteem all, defy no one,
for no reason affront anyone.*
WORDS OF AN AZTEC NOBLEMAN TO HIS SONS[1]

Saint Augustine wrote, "What then is time? If no one asks
me, I know what it is. If I wish to explain it to him who
asks, I do not know."

The abstract nature of time truly does make it difficult
to define. However, many earlier cultures learned to relate to
time in spiritual ways that helped them to understand it and
develop a personal relationship with it. They truly seemed to
"know" time much better than we do.

In this chapter you will become aware of how some
Mesoamerican cultures (the Toltecs, Itza-Maya, and Aztecs)
defined time. Their findings are likely to intrigue you and
keep you wondering. As you will see, these people trusted in
the prophecies they were given.

What do you think about their prophecies concerning the future? Will you learn to relate to time as they did?

THE MESOAMERICAN WORLD VIEW

As we have already mentioned, most ancient cultures placed high value on prophecy. We've seen this in the civilizations of the Mayans and the Incas. The Mayans predicted that December 21, 2012, will be the last day of history as we know it, and the Q'ero Inca shamans also prophesied that great change will take place around the same time.

December 21, 2012!

What we have learned about the Mayans and the Q'ero people in the first two chapters of this book give us great insights into the world views of these indigenous cultures, and many of these viewpoints were shared by the Toltecs, Itza-Mayans, and Aztecs.

In the Aztec father's advice to his sons (in the epigraph at the beginning of this chapter) we find great wisdom, and we gain understanding of the core values of the Mesoamericans: respect for God and other people, humility, hope in God, and peace. The Mayans, Incas, Toltecs, Itza-Mayans, Aztecs, and other Mesoamericans endeavored to cultivate these concepts within their given cultures, and they have expressed a desire to see these incorporated into the lives and cultures of people everywhere.

The Aztec father's powerful words resound with impact in our hearts today. If his advice were heeded, would many of mankind's problems be resolved? Is there anything in his words that does not apply to our lives today? Could we use his admonition to his sons as moral teaching for children today?

Clearly, the values of love and compassion, along with a deep respect for nature, were integral to the religious philosophies and mythologies of these different groups. For instance, all of them believed in mankind's interdependence with nature.

In all likelihood, trade between cultures in the regions we now call Central and South America caused some cross-pollination to take place with regard to religion, philosophy, prophecy, a view of history and eschatology, and other matters. Many times we find close commonalities among all Mesoamerican cultures with regard to each of these topics.

For example, each of these cultures closely observed the cycles of nature. Often, these cycles involved destruction followed by rebirth. In determining these cycles, these ancient cultures employed sophisticated science and mathematics, resulting in precise reckonings with regard to time and its eras.

It is interesting to note that modern science has confirmed many of their speculations with regard to the cycles of nature—specific eras in which the planet underwent drastic and cataclysmic changes. There is evidence to suggest that global changes in climate and other factors, such as floods, meteors, volcanoes, polar shifts, and changes in temperature, may have caused the demise of previous Earth cycles, as these cultures have suggested.

As a case in point, some scientists believe that a cosmic body passed the Earth approximately twelve thousand years ago, and this caused major climate changes on the planet that resulted in the death of most life forms. On another occasion a polar shift may have led to the near-extinction of life on our planet. It is also theorized that a meteor striking the Earth and a massive volcanic eruption caused the disruption of life, as well.

Are we living in Earth's final cycle? Let's see what the Toltecs, Itza-Mayans, and Aztecs had to say.

QUETZALCOATL

THE TOLTECS

The Toltecs lived in Mexico from AD 800 to AD 1200. They were among the first people to become experts in metallurgy, and they created metal sculptures from copper and gold. They were also masters in architecture, and they constructed long-lasting temples and pyramids.

Originally, the Toltecs were very militaristic, and they endeavored to dominate their neighbors through military might.

Like the Mayans and the Incas, the Toltecs were polytheistic, and they practiced ritual sacrifices of human beings in order to appease the gods and atone for their sins.

Though there are many unanswered questions about their demise, it appears that the downfall of the Toltecs may have resulted from internal conflicts between two different factions that had conflicting ideologies. One of these factions worshiped and followed a militaristic deity, while the other gave allegiance to a more peaceful god. This division, along with plagues and the immigration of other tribes from the North, left the Toltecs vulnerable and defenseless.

Though they were not as powerful in some ways as the Mayans and the Incas were, the Toltecs definitely left their mark upon later civilizations, including the Aztecs, who eventually conquered them.

TOLTEC PROPHECIES ABOUT QUETZALCOATL

The ancient prophet-ruler of the Toltecs was Quetzalcoatl. He was known as "the plumed serpent." His essential message was one of love and respect, a value he held so high that it led him to forbid the practice of human sacrifices, which were quite common among other tribes.

Quetzalcoatl was described as being a white man with a beard, and he wore long robes. He preached about the one supreme God, and he developed a calendar for his people. When he left the Toltec people due to the fact that he was displeased and dissatisfied over their enmity and violence and the way they treated powerful religious leaders, he promised he would return one day.

The people believed that Quetzalcoatl left Mexico by boat toward the West—via the Pacific Ocean. They believed he would return by boat from the East. In fact, Quetzalcoatl prophesied that he would return from across the vast sea (the Atlantic Ocean).[2]

Some have interpreted this prophecy to mean that the prophet's spiritual message about love, respect, and unity,

2012: IS THIS THE END?

rather than the man himself, would one day return by way of another great prophet. Others believed (and some still believe) in a literal bodily return of Quetzalcoatl.

Dr. Herbert Josph Spinden calls Quetzalcoatal, "... perhaps the most remarkable figure in ancient American history."[3] He bases this statement on the fact that the prophet-ruler was both a great religious leader and a practical teacher, one who taught his people about the arts, science, and useful social customs. Some have compared Quetzalcoatal to Saint Thomas; others have even compared him to Jesus Christ.

It is believed that Quetzalcoatl established the Toltec Era on August 16, 1168. Interestingly, most Mexican year counts begin with that date. A Toltec Era was considered to be fifty-two years long, and both the Toltec and Aztec calendars were based on cycles of fifty-two years. Their year was of the same length as ours, but the Mayan year that we referred to earlier was shorter than ours by five days.[4]

What do the ancient prophecies have to say about the return of Quetzalcoatl? It is believed that he will return during the thirteenth Toltec Era. Based on their calendar, that era could not take place prior to AD 1844. Coincidentally, 1844 was the year when the Millerites (forerunners of present-day Seventh-Day Adventists) believed Christ would return. (They based this belief on their interpretation of Daniel 8:13-14 and Matthew 24:15.)[5]

We are now in the thirteenth Toltec Era—the prophesied time of great change and upheaval.

Are the changes and upheavals that society is currently facing tied in with this prophecy? Were the Toltecs right? Is Quetzalcoatl about to return? Who is Quetzalcoatl?

CHILAM-BALAM OF THE ITZA-MAYA

The stimulus for the establishment of the New Mayan Empire (from around AD 1000 to AD 1350) was largely based on the Nahuatl-speaking people from central Mexico—the Itzas. They were related to or had descended from the Toltecs, and they held strongly to the belief in Quetzalcoatl and his prophecies.

It was around the year AD 1500 that a famous seer named Chilam-Balam appeared among the Itza-Maya people. He foretold the coming of the white man to the New World and warned the people that these "strange visitors" would bring devastating diseases and war to their region. His prophecies, which were based on the Mayan calendar, came true.

The prophecies of Chilam-Balam were recorded in a book that is now entitled *Book of the Jaguar Priest*, but was originally entitled *The Book of Chilam-Balam of Tizimin*. This volume is filled with extraordinary prophecies, such as the prophecy that the Itza-Maya people would suffer greatly under the rule of the white man. However, he went on to offer them hope by saying that their ancient glory would one day be restored as the result of a new religion that would bring the whole world into harmony.[6]

The story of Chilam-Balam provides us with further evidence that prophecy was very important to these early Mesoamerican people. When the Spaniards came to Mexico in 1519, many of the natives thought that the Spanish leader Hernando Cortez was the reincarnation of Quetzalcoatl—a return that had long been prophesied.

THE AZTEC EMPIRE

Like other Mesoamericans before them, the Aztecs believed that the Earth had been created and destroyed several times. Their mythology held that great death and destruction had taken place at the end of each of the previous worlds. They also believed that the sun had been created and destroyed on four different occasions:

1. The first sun was destroyed by water—a great deluge.

TENOCHTITLAN

2. The second sun was destroyed by wind.
3. The third sun was destroyed by fire.
4. The fourth sun was destroyed by a rain of fire and blood.

The Aztecs and other Mesoamericans based their understanding of these cycles on their observation of the heavens and the ongoing process of death and rebirth in nature. Spring—the time of new life—follows winter—the time of death and destruction.

Similarly, the end of one world leads to the rebirth of a new world (or new age).

This leads us to ask: When will our present world come to an end? What will happen afterward?

The Aztecs have given some answers to these questions, as you will see in the remainder of this chapter.

GAINING STRENGTH THROUGH UNITY

The Aztecs built their culture on a foundation that had been laid by the Toltecs. Like their predecessors, they strongly believed in prophecy and in intimacy with nature. They arrived in Mexico from the north in about AD 1248. They settled near Lake Texcoco and established the great city of Tenochtitlan nearby. Using what they had learned from the Toltecs, they were able to turn the marshy land of that vicinity into firm, arable soil.

This city was vast and beautiful, and it was filled with temples and gardens.

At first the Aztec culture was somewhat weak and vulnerable, but in time, under their chiefs, Itzcoatle and Moctezuma II, and through an alliance with neighboring states, they were able to overcome their enemies. This caused other tribes to respect and honor them.

However, when the Spaniards under the leadership of Hernando Cortez arrived near the present-day city of Vera

Cruz in November of 1519, the conquistadors were able to find and enter the city of Tenochtitlan with little difficulty.

THE CONQUISTADORS

Why were the Spaniards able to conquer the Aztecs so quickly? There are several conceivable answers to this question, but the role of prophecy in the Aztec culture is, in all likelihood, a key factor. Prior to the arrival of Cortez, the Aztecs had observed many different phenomena in the heavens. They interpreted these to be signs that their kingdom was on the verge of collapse.

For example, they witnessed several comets, and from this they determined that two of their temples would be destroyed. In addition to these prophecies of doom, it is interesting to note that Cortez arrived during the time of the harvest—a time when the Aztecs were not prepared for war, because their focus was solely on the reaping of the harvest.

Certain of their enemies, the Tiaxcalans in particular, joined with Cortez in his fight against the Aztecs, as well. All of these factors, mixed with the belief that Quetzalcoatl was soon to return (to destroy the Aztec Empire), caused these people to be very vulnerable and defenseless.

THE LIGHTING OF THE NEW AGE

The Toltec legends told of Quetzalcoatl, a white-skinned, bearded priest who would come from the East to establish an enlightened kingdom among the Indians. This view of the future was supported by Nezhaulcoyotl, a king of Texcoco, whose reign bridged the fifteenth and sixteenth centuries. He was a great astrologer who had an observatory built on the roof of his palace.

When Moctezuma II (aka Montezuma II) was elected King of Mexico, Nezhaulcoytl praised the nation for choosing a ruler "... whose deep knowledge of heavenly things insured to his subjects his comprehension of those of an earthly nature."[7]

Nezhaulcoytl gave the king detailed warnings of a new astrological age that was beginning according to the Aztec calendar. One omen of this was a famine that took place during 1507. This was followed by an earthquake that occurred after the "Lighting of the New Age" ceremony that Moctezuma II had inaugurated. It was felt that these omens were signs of impending disaster, as well.

Each year thereafter, until Cortez arrived, a new omen appeared. A comet with three heads and sparks shooting from its tail was observed. Another comet in a later year was described as follows: "... a pyramidal light, which scattered sparks on all sides, rose at midnight from the eastern horizon till the apex reached the zenith and faded at dawn." This same phenomenon recurred for forty nights, and it was interpreted as being prophetic of "... wars, famines, pestilence, and mortality among the lords."[8]

As you can see, the Aztec people had begun to anticipate hard times, and they were preparing for the worst. They expected all kinds of bad things to happen, and their expectations were soon realized. Was this a self-fulfilling prophecy? Or was it a form of fate that could not be avoided?

In 1508, Moctezuma II visited Tillancalmecatl (the "Place of Heavenly Learning"), where he was given a rare bird. He reported that he saw stars and "fire sticks" within the bird's shiny crest. (It is believed that the "fire sticks" he saw were a prophetic vision of the guns that were carried by the conquistadors.) Then the image changed to show the advance of warriors riding on horses, which the emperor described as deer, since he had never seen a horse.

In the same year the emperor's sister Paranazin collapsed into a cataleptic trance that was mistaken for death. She recovered while the funeral procession was taking her to the royal crypt. She said that during her time of unconsciousness —

a trance-like state—she received a vision of great ships arriving from a distant land. She went on to describe white men who were wearing metal "casques" (helmets), holding banners, and carrying "fire sticks."[9]

For several days during 1519—the year the conquistadors arrived—a comet was observed over the city of Tenochtitlan. The Aztecs described it as, "… a rip in the sky which bleeds celestial influences drop-wise onto the Aztec world." Soon thereafter a thunderbolt struck the temple of the deity Huitilopchitle, and the building was burned to the ground.[10]

These and many other signs convinced the Aztecs that their doom had been ordained, sealed, and announced by celestial powers. It is truly remarkable that Cortez's ship landed on the precise date that the Aztec calendar had calculated for the return of Quetzalcoatl. It was the end of the period that they called the 13th Heaven (from the Thirteen Heavens of Decreasing Choice) and the beginning of what they called the Nine Hells (of Increasing Doom).

From their point of view, actual historical figures were acting out the events that had long been prophesied.

THE NEW BIRTH AND THE NEW CAREER

Though nearly overwhelmed by his superstitious fear of the mythic Quetzalcoatl, Moctezuma II is said to have greeted Cortez at the city gates with these words: "O lord, with what trouble have you journeyed to reach us, have arrived in this land, your own country of Mexico, to sit on your throne, which I have been guarding for you this while; I have been watching for you, for my ancestors told that you would return. Welcome to this land. Rest awhile; rest in your palace."[11]

Although Cortez was outnumbered militarily by more than a thousand to one (Moctezuma's palace guard alone was larger than Cortez's entire expedition), he boldly accepted the emperor's offer. The Spaniard proceeded to capture

Moctezuma and display the king to his subjects. Reacting in anger, the people stoned and fatally wounded their king. The Aztec Empire fell soon afterward.

As he lay dying, Moctezuma had a wondrous vision, which he shared with his favorite daughter, Tula. She later shared his vision with the Tezcucan noble Iztlilzochitl, who recorded it as follows: "To the world I have said farewell. I see its vanities go away from me one by one. Last in the train and most loved, most glittering is power, and in its hands I see my heart. A shadow creeps over me, darkening all without, but brightening all within, and in the brightness, lo, I see my people and their future! The long, long cycles, two, four, eight, pass away, and I see the tribes newly risen, like the trodden grass, and in their midst a priesthood and a cross. An age of battle more, and lo, there remains the cross, but not the priests; in their stead is freedom and God. I know the children of the Aztecs, crushed now, will live, and more after ages suffered by them, they will rise up, and take their place—a place of splendor—amongst the deathless nations of the earth. What I was given to see was revelation. Cherish these words, O Tula; repeat them often, make them a cry of the people, a sacred tradition; let them go down with the generations, one of which will, at last, understand the meaning of the words freedom and God, now dark to my understanding; and then, not till then, will be the new birth and new career."[12]

Was the emperor witnessing (in his spirit) a future Christian revival that would be centered on the cross and would result in greater spiritual freedom and peace?

THE EAGLE BOWL—THE AZTEC CALENDAR

The sacred Aztec Calendar (or Mexica sun stone—stone of the sun) is also known as the Eagle Bowl. It is a large monolithic sculpture that was excavated in Mexico City in 1790. It is an amazingly accurate calendar that has been in

SUN STONE—AZTEC CALENDAR

existence for more than two thousand years. The calendar was dedicated to the solar deity Tonatiuh, who was believed to be the fifth sun god, as a means to prevent further catastrophe by performing human sacrifices in his honor.[13]

A Zapotec prophecy that is based on the Eagle Bowl states: "After Thirteen Heavens of Decreasing Choice, and Nine Hells of Increasing Doom, the Tree of Life shall blossom with a fruit never before known in the creation, and that fruit shall be the New Spirit of Men."[14]

Aztec mythology states that the first age of mankind ended with animals devouring humans. The second age was finished by wind. The third was destroyed by fire, and the fourth by water.

According to their reckoning, we are now living in the fifth epoch, which is known as Nahui-Olin (Sun of Earthquake). The fifth epoch began in 3113 BC, and it will end either in December 2011, or December 2012. (There is some confusion regarding the precise end date, but note its similarity to the Mayan predictions of the end of time.)

Whichever date is the final one, the Aztecs believe it will be the final day of human existence on Earth. The important thing to realize here is that this predicted "final day" is prophesied to occur in the very near future.

THE FIFTH SUN—THE SUN OF MOVEMENT

The Aztecs, like many Mesoamericans, believed it was possible to predict the future by studying the past. They also believed that fate and/or destiny could not be altered.

Each sun that is depicted on the Aztec calendar (sun stone) is a period identified with certain events that brought each period to an end. It appears that they believe that our present age will end with massive earthquakes, because the fifth sun is known as "the sun of movement." This stage will end as a result of the Earth's movement (earthquakes). Again, the precise date of this cataclysm is not known, but there is every reason to believe that it coincides fairly closely with the Mayan predictions related to December 21, 2012.

A valuable document that has been preserved is the *Codex Vaticanus*. It describes the four stages the Earth has already gone though:

"**First Sun, 'Matlactli Atl':** duration 4,008 years. Those who lived then ate water maize called 'atsitzintli.' In this age lived the giants....The First Sun was destroyed by water in the sign 'Matlactli Atl' (Ten Water). It was called 'Apachiohualiztli' (flood, deluge), the art of sorcery of the permanent rain. Men were turned into fish. Some say that only one couple escaped, protected by an old tree living near the water. Others say that there were seven couples who hid in a cave until the flood was over and the waters had gone down. They repopulated the Earth and were worshipped as gods in their nations....

"**Second Sun, 'Ehecoatl':** duration 4,010 years. Those who lived then ate wild fruit known as 'acotzintli.' This Sun was destroyed by Ehecoatl (Winged Serpent) and men were turned into monkeys.... One man and one woman, standing on a rock, were saved from destruction....

"**Third Sun, 'Tleyquiyahuillo':** duration 4,081 years. Men, the descendants of the couple who were saved from the Second Sun, ate a fruit called 'tzincoacoc.' This Third Sun was destroyed by fire.

"**Fourth Sun, Tzontillic:** duration 5,026 years. Men died of starvation after a deluge of blood and fire.... "[15]

Now we are living in the Fifth Sun — the Sun of Movement — and it is prophesied to be the age that will end with massive earthquakes. In this connection, it is interesting to note these words of Jesus about the end times: *"Nation shall rise against nation, and kingdom against kingdom. And great earthquakes shall be in divers places, and famines, and pestilences; and fearful sights and great signs shall there be from heaven"* (Luke 21:10-11, KJV).

How do we test a prophecy or a prophet? The real test is found in whether the prophecies come true. Many of the prophecies of these early peoples did come true, and this brought tumultuous changes to their lives. Will their prophecies about our future have the same impact upon us?

"Time is the most undefinable yet paradoxical of things; the past is gone, the future is not come, and the present becomes the past even while we attempt to define it, and, like the flash of lightning, at once exists and expires" (Charles Caleb Colton).

ENDNOTES

1. *Prophecies of the Toltecs and Mayas.* http://www.bci.org/prophecy-fulfilled/mayan.htm
2. Ibid.
3. Ibid.
4. Ibid.
5. Ibid.
6. Ibid.
7. *The Prophecies of South America.* http://www.alternativeapproaches.com/magick/sap/sap2.htm
8. Ibid.
9. Ibid.
10. Ibid.
11. Ibid.
12. Ibid.
13. *The End of the World,* compiled by Dee Finney. http://www.greatdreams.com/end-world.htm
14. Ibid.

15. *When Will the World End—2012?* http://www.redicecreations.
com/specialreports/2006/1Oct/worldend2012.html

Other Resources That Were Consulted in the Preparation of This Chapter

1. *Toltecs.* http://www.mnsu.edu/emuseum/prehistory/
latinamerica/meso/cultures/toltec.html
2. *Toltec.* http://en.wikipedia.org/wiki/Toltec
3. http://www.professorfringe.com/pp_prophecies/toltec_mayas_
proph.htm
4. *Aztec Calendar Stone.* http://en.wikipedia.org/wiki/Aztec_
sun_stone
5. *Mayan Aztec Prophecies.* http://www.apocalypse-soon.com/
mayan_aztec_prophecies.htm
6. http://www.december212012.com/articles/religion/Biblical-
Response.htm
7. *The Civilization of the Toltecs.* http://www.stockton,edu/
~gilmorew/consorti/1gcenso.htm
8. *Don't Forget: the End of the World Is in Four Years.* http://
www.socyberty.com/Paranormal/Dont-Forget-The-End-of-
the-World-is-in-Four-Years.htm
9. *A Short Study of End Time Prophecies.* http://www.angelfire.
com/music2/fullcircle/PropheciesStudy.html

Additional Resources You May Wish to Explore

1. *The Toltec Heritage: From the Fall of Tula to the Rise of
Tenochtitlan* by Nigel Davies. Published by the University of
Oklahoma Press, 1980.
2. *The Gods and Symbols of Ancient Mexico and the Maya* by
Mary Miller and Karl Taube. Published by Thames & Hudson,
1993.

4

THE BOOK OF CHANGES— THE *I CHING*

When the way comes to an end, then change.
Having changed, you pass through.
I CHING

Change is certain. Peace is followed by disturbances;
departure of evil men by their return. Such recurrences
should not constitute occasions for sadness but for
awareness, so that one may be happy in the interim.
I CHING

The *I Ching* is known as the book of changes. As time passes, changes always occur. Are you a friend of time, or is time your enemy?

How do you deal with change? Are you afraid of change, or do you embrace it with zeal?

Do you find the changes of life to be threatening, or exciting?

The wisdom that is found in the *I Ching* might help you understand the changes that come with the passage of time in a new way.

Charles Caleb Colton wrote, "Time, the cradle of hope.... Wisdom walks before it, opportunity with it, and repentance behind it; he that has made it his friend will have little to fear from his enemies, but he that has made it his enemy will have little to hope from his friends."

In this chapter you will learn how the Chinese culture made time its friend, and you will discover, also, what this culture had to say about the future.

WISDOM FROM ONE OF THE OLDEST BOOKS IN THE WORLD

The *I Ching* (also known as the *Yi King*) is a Chinese book that is approximately five thousand years old. Its title means "Book of Changes" or "Classic of Changes." The theme of this ancient work deals with the dynamic balance of opposites, the evolution of events as a process, and the acceptance of the inevitability of change.

Yes, change is a constant certainty, and it seems as if the speed of change in the world is increasing with each passing day. Take a look at some of the changes that have occurred since humans began domesticating plants and animals several thousand years ago:

• The printing press was invented approximately five hundred years ago.

• We began driving automobiles about one hundred years ago.

• The computer was invented about fifty years ago.

• Men landed on the moon in 1969—forty years ago.

Everything is increasing at an accelerating (if not alarming) pace, and things will continue to change—probably even more quickly than they do now. Technology advances at such a rapid rate that it is difficult to keep pace with it. We may even have human clones in the near future, and many other new medical developments appear to be right around the corner.

Some have said that the time will come when the rate of change will speed up so much that all that will remain is change. When this happens, we will have reached the point of infinity (the zero state), and many believe this will take place sometime after 2010.

Mathematicians use the term "singularity" to describe a point when an equation breaks down and ceases to have any useful meaning. Some, such as the futurist and inventor Ray Kurzweil, who wrote *The Singularity Is Near*, believes that if the power of computers keeps on doubling every eighteen months, there will eventually be a computer that can equal the human brain.[1]

If his prediction comes true, will there be a computer sometime in the near future that will surpass the capabilities of the human brain? If so, at that point there will be no need for humans to develop new computers, because machines will invent better ones than we ever could, and they would be able to do so much more quickly than we ever could.

Peter Russell writes, "What happens then? is a big question. Some propose that humans would become obsolete; machines would become the vanguard of evolution. Others think there would be a merging of human and machine intelligence— downloading our minds into computers, perhaps."[2]

These speculations have become fodder for several science fiction novels and motion pictures. However, if there is any possibility that these predictions could come true, the world of the future will be radically different from our present reality. Will machines take over everything? Is such a scenario even possible?

Let's see what two men who studied the *I Ching* had to say.

THE ORACLES OF THE I CHING

A team of two brothers closely studied the *I Ching*. These men—Terence and Dennis McKenna—are known as ethnobotanists and fractal time experts.

As a result of their studies, the McKennas believed that December 21, 2012, is the exact point when humanity will

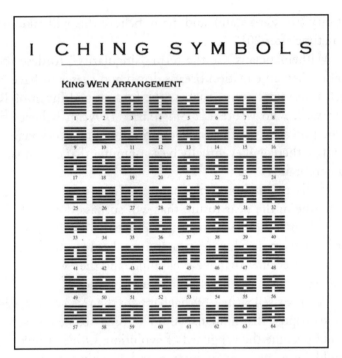

THE I CHING SYMBOLS

THE TAOISM YIN AND YANG SYMBOL

reach infinity (what they call the zero state). Their studies of this potential future phenomenon are based in part on their analysis of the symbols found in the *I Ching*—a study they conducted early in the seventies with no knowledge of the Mayan calendar. (Their book, *The Invisible Landscape*, was published in 1973.)[3]

The text of *The Book of Changes* (the *I Ching*) involves prophetic statements and words of wisdom; some of these are represented by a set of sixty-four abstract line arrangements known as hexagrams, or six-line figures. Each hexagram represents the description of a particular state or process.

These hexagrams are developed from gradations of binary expressions that are based on the Taoist concepts of *yin* and *yang*. The yang is the creative principle, which is represented by solid lines. The yin is the receptive principle, and it is represented by broken lines.[4]

The McKenna brothers took the number six from the six-line figures (hexagrams) and multiplied it times the number of the different arrangements of these figures—sixty-four in all, as follows: 6 X 64 = 384, a number which is exceptionally close to the exact number of days in thirteen lunar months. As a result, they and many others feel that the *I Ching* is actually an ancient Chinese calendar.

At the risk of oversimplifying the very complex mathematics involved in the McKennas' calculations, let's take a closer look at some of their conclusions:

• 1 day X 64 X 6 = 384 days = 13 lunar months
• 384 days X 64 = 67 years (104.25 days) = 6 minor sunspot cycles of 11.2 years each
• 67 years (104.25 days) X 64 = 4,306 + years = 2 Zodiacal ages
• 4,306 + years X 6 = 25,836 years = 1 precession of the equinoxes. (Refer to Chapter 1 for more about the precession of the equinoxes.)

Note the similarity of their findings to the understanding of the Mesoamericans that was based on the precise Mayan calendar. The McKennas matched the levels of the *I Ching* pattern with key periods in history. Through complicated mathematical calculations (using fractals — rough or fragmented geometric shapes that can be split into parts, each of which is, at least approximately, a reduced-size copy of the whole) they determined that everything would fit best if the end-of-time scale were set at December 21-22, 2012.[5]

They used the base period of sixty-seven years in the following overview of history: (Please bear in mind that the dates they have pinpointed for certain events are not accepted by many.)

• 2012 minus 67 years = 1945, which was a year of great change on Earth, including the ending of World War II and the dropping of atomic bombs on Hiroshima and Nagasaki.

• 2012 minus 4,300 years (67 X 64) = 2300 BC, the approximate beginning of historical time; the development of civilizations.

• 2012 minus 275,000 years (4,300 X 64) = the presumed emergence of human beings.

• 2012 minus 18 million years (275,000 X 64) = the peak of the age of mammals.

• 2012 minus 1.3 billion years = the presumed beginning of life on this planet.[6]

Here is what the McKenna brothers have to say about what will happen when the next base period of sixty-seven years rolls around in the year 2012:

"Achievement of the zero state can be imagined to arrive in one of two forms. One is the dissolution of the cosmos in an actual cessation and unraveling of the natural laws, a literal apocalypse. The other possibility, the culmination of a human process, a process of tool making, which comes to completion in the perfect artifact: the monadic self, exteriorized, condensed, and visible in three dimensions; in alchemical terms. The dream of a union of spirit and matter."[7]

Will a destructive Apocalypse take place on December 21, 2012, or will we enter an entirely new phase of existence—the union of spirit and matter?

What will happen to us?

TIMEWAVE ZERO

To explain the McKennas' theory more fully, let's take a look at their concept that is known as "the timewave." This idea is similar to the one that was advanced by Alfred North Whitehead, which he called the "ingression of novelty."[8] Both the timewave and the ingression of novelty refer to new forms and new developments that come into existence at increasingly rapid rates.

The McKennas' timewave is not a smooth curve. Rather, it has highs and lows that relate to the patterns of new developments throughout history. This curve shows a rise in novelty that took place around 500 BC (the era during which men like Lao Tzu, Plato, Buddha, and other leaders unveiled their philosophies).

The McKennas show that the same pattern emerged during the 1960's, but during that decade it occurred sixty-four times faster than earlier rises in novelty did. According to them the pattern will be repeated in 2010 at a rate that is sixty-four times faster than the preceding one. They predict that it will repeat again in 2012, sixty-four times faster again.

The accelerating pattern will, according to the McKennas, one day reach "Timewave Zero."[9] They believed, as we said before, that this point would be reached on December 21, 2012.

The Timewave Zero concept is also known as the Novelty Theory. This theory attempts to calculate the ebb and flow of novelty in the universe as an inherent quality of time. The word "novelty" in this context refers to newness and dynamic change. According to the McKennas and several others, these fluctuations of change can be graphed throughout human history.[10]

This theory was revised by a nuclear physicist named John Sheliak.[11] His relatively new revision is sometimes referred to as Timewave One. It is believed that Sheliak's version is more closely matched to history than the McKenna brothers' approach was.

Here are the basic tenets of these timewave theories:

• The universe is a living system with a teleological attractor at the end of time that drives the increase and conservation of energy in material forms. (Teleology deals with the philosophical study of design and purpose.)

• Novelty and complexity increase over time.

• The human brain represents the pinnacle of complex organization in the universe.

• Fluctuations in novelty are self-similar at different scales. For example, the rise and fall of the Roman Empire could be seen as being similar to the life of a family within a single generation, or even with an individual's typical workday.

• As the complexity and sophistication of human thought and culture increase, universal novelty approaches a curve of exponential growth.

• Immediately prior to and during this omega point of infinite novelty, anything and everything conceivable to the human mind will occur simultaneously.

• The end point of all this is seen as being December 21, 2012.[12]

Terence McKenna describes a great acceleration of human cultural development, which he compares to a "tightening spiral." He describes this process as being mankind and the universe approaching the "transcendental object of the universe."[13]

Other philosophers have agreed with him. One of these is Ray Kurzweil who developed a theory that is known as "The Law of Accelerating Returns."[14] Likewise, Stuart Kauffman developed a concept that is known as "The Adjacent Possible."[15]

Another philosopher, Robert Anton Wilson, has put forth a theory that he called, "The Jumping Jesus Phenomenon" in a seminar that was entitled, "The Acceleration of Knowledge." He explains that knowledge has doubled over history and that these doublings are occurring more rapidly as time goes forth.[16]

Certainly, these men are accurate with regard to the speeding up of the acquisition of knowledge and the many changes that are associated with each new development. It will be interesting to see what new things will happen next.

A Monument of Antiquity

In the later years of his life Confucius said, "If some years were added to my life, I would give fifty to the study of the Yi [the *I Ching*], and might then escape falling into great errors."[17]

This ancient text, which some believe is the oldest book in the world, has occupied the attention of scholars throughout history. The roots of both Confucianism and Taoism are found in this book, and much of Chinese culture has been inspired by it.

Though the authorship of this book is not certain, many believe it was written by the legendary Chinese Emperor Fu Hsi (2953-2838 BC). Some of the appendices were added by Confucius, a Chinese philosopher who lived approximately twenty-five hundred years ago.

As the following excerpts reveal, Confucius was a wise man whose proverbs continue to be respected and followed:

• Wherever you go, go with all your heart.

THE CHINESE PHILOSOPHER CONFUCIUS

• What you do not wish upon yourself, extend not to others.
• Everything has its beauty, but not everyone sees it.
• If you shoot for the stars and hit the moon, it's OK. But you've got to shoot for something. A lot of people don't even shoot.
• When you are laboring for others, let it be with the same zeal as if it were for yourself.
• Our greatest glory is not in never failing, but in rising every time we fail.
• The cautious seldom err.
• Choose a job you love and you will never have to work a day in your life.
• Life is really simple, but we insist on making it complicated.

Confucius invented the fortune cookie in the early fifth century BC. His concept was to create a cookie that provided both physical and mental/spiritual nourishment. The fortunes contained within the cookies are words of prophetic wisdom— general prophecies that make direct application to daily living. Here is an example of one such fortune: "Strong-willed is he who tests himself against the mighty waters."[18]

ORDER IN RANDOM EVENTS

Ancient Chinese philosophy sought to find order in random events and this is reflected in the *I Ching*. The text of the ancient classic describes a system of cosmology and philosophy that helped form the Chinese culture.

Many consider the *I Ching* to be a system of divination through which the future may be told both for individuals and humanity in general. Individuals who are seeking answers engage in a process of divination that is known as "casting the *I Ching*."

The word "*I*" or "*Yi*" is a verb that means "to change" or "to exchange/substitute one thing for another." It also implies "ease, simplicity, transformation, and invariability."

The word "*Ching*" or "*Jing*" means "regularity" or "persistency." Hence, *I Ching* or *Yi Jing* refers to the regularity of change in life.

When we examine these definitions more closely, we begin to understand Chinese philosophy more fully. For example, simplicity is seen as the root of substance. It is perceived as being a fundamental law underlying everything in the universe. Everything is seen as being utterly plain and simple, no matter how complicated or complex it might appear to be on the surface.

The word "variability" refers to how we use substance. Everything in the universe is seen as constantly changing. This view helps us to understand the importance of flexibility in life and enables us to deal more effectively with the many diverse situations that may come up.

In the word "persistency" we find the essence of substance. While everything in the universe continues to change, there remains a persistent principle or a central rule upon which we can focus. This principle, or focal point, does not vary with either space or time.

The ancient Chinese viewed the *I Ching* as having two distinct functions:

1. It is a compendium of ancient cosmic principles.
2. It is a text of divination.

It is the second function that arouses our interest in this book. The Chinese firmly believed that the future results of our actions were determined by our personal virtues.

In light of this concept we can see that the *I Ching's* apparent prophecy about the end of time is tied in directly with the way humans have behaved through the centuries. It is, therefore, a collective prophecy that applies to humanity in general.

We are living in a time when many people are sensing that a great change is about to take place. Some are entering this phase of the human experience with fear and trepidation, while others are approaching it with hope and optimism. What makes the difference? As you continue to read, you will gain new understandings about the future, and you will learn how to put your fears about the future to rest.

Thomas Hardy wrote, "Time changes everything except something within us which is always surprised by change."

According to the *I Ching*, many surprising changes lie ahead. Will you be surprised, challenged, or frightened by them? The choice is yours.

Is the destruction of humanity just around the corner, or are we getting ready to realize our full potential as human beings? Are we on the verge of the Apocalypse, or are we living in the eve of a recovered paradise on Earth?

Are you ready for the inevitable changes that lie ahead?

"The only constant is change, continuing change, inevitable change, that is the dominant factor in society today. No sensible decision can be made any longer without taking into account not only the world as it is, but the world as it will be" (Isaac Asimov).

ENDNOTES

1. *Raymond Kurzweil.* En.wikipedia.org/wiki/Ray_Kurzweil
2. Russell, Peter, *The Mystery of 2012*—"A Singularity in Time." Sounds True, Inc., Boulder, Colorado, 2007.
3. Ibid.
4. *I Ching—End of the World—December 21, 2012.* http://www. liveindia.com/mayacalendar/iching.html
5. Ibid.

6. Ibid.

7. Ibid.

8. Russell, Peter, *The Mystery of 2012* — "A Singularity in Time." Sounds True, Inc., Boulder, Colorado, 2007.

9. Ibid.

10. Ibid.

11. *The Zero Date* by Peter Meyer. www.hermetic.ch/Frt/zerodate.html

12. Ibid.

13. *Timewave Zero and Language* by Terence McKenna. Users.lycaeum.org/~sputnik/mckenna/TZandL.html

14. *Accelerating Change.* en.wikipedia.org/wiki/Accelerating_change

15. *The Adjacent Possible. A Talk With Stuart Kauffman. Edge Video.* www.comdig.org/index.php?id_issue=2003.45

16. *Timewave Zero.* en.wikipedia.org/wiki/Novelty_theory

17. http://www.sacred-texts.com/ich/icintr01.htm

18. *Fortune Cookie.* http://uncyclopeida.wikia.com/wiki/Fortune_Cookie

Other Resources That Were Consulted in the Preparation of This Chapter

1. *Confucius Quotes.* http://thinkexist.com/confucius_quotes/

2. *I Ching Quotes and Quotations.* http://www.sayings-quotes.com/i_ching_quotes/

3. http://www.gaia.com/quotes/I_Ching

4. *2012 Warning.* http://www.2012warning.com/i-ching-2012.htm

5. *Survive 2012* — "Fractal Time and the I Ching." http://www.survive2012.com/why_2012_fractal.php

6. http://www.december212012.com/articles/reviews/2012_Are_you_ready.htm

7. *The World Will End in 2012, Say Experts.* http://www.merinews.com/catFull.jsp?articleID=139440

8. http://www.sacred-texts.com/ich/index.htm

9. *Yi Jing—I Ching, the Book of Changes.* http://afpc.asso.fr/wengu/wg/wengu.php?l=Yijing
10. *I Ching Wisdom.* http://www.ichingwisdom.com/IChingWisdom/index.html
11. *2012 Predictions Review.* http://2012-predictions-review.blogspot.com/2008/01/i-ching

Additional Resources You May Wish to Explore

1. http://www.gaia.com/quotes/I_Ching
2. http://thinkexist.com/quotes/i_ching
3. http://www.2012warning.com/i-ching-2012.htm
4. *The Mandate of Heaven: Hidden History in the I Ching* by S.J. Marshall. Published by Columbia University Press, New York, 2001.
5. *Zhouyi: the Book of Changes* by R. Rutt, Curzon Press, 1996.
6. *Fathoming the Cosmos and Ordering the World: The Yijing* by Richard J. Smith. Published by University of Virginia Press, 2008.

5

HOPI INDIAN PROPHECIES

When the Blue Star Kachina makes its appearance in the heavens, the Fifth World will emerge.
FROM AN ANCIENT HOPI PROPHECY[1]

One must learn a different ... sense of time, one that depends more on small amounts than big ones.
SISTER MARY PAUL

Divisions of time into cycles and eras, both big and small, have provided many cultures with what they believe are glimpses into the future. For example, the *I Ching* and the Mesoamericans have taught that one cycle morphs into a new cycle. They believe that these patterns are repeated over and over again until the end of the age. The fact is that things do change, as mankind goes from one age to the next.

The Hopi Indians certainly held to this point of view, as well. In this chapter you will see how their culture's sense of time was very different from our own. You will also see how closely their concepts correlate with those of other ancient cultures.

This Native American culture envisions a fifth world. Has it already begun? Many Hopis suggest that the end is near.

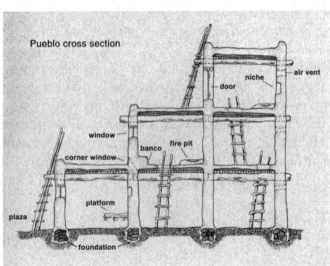

A HOPI PUEBLO

THE HOPI PEOPLE

The name "Hopi" means "good, peaceful, and wise." Another translation of the name is: "People who live in the correct way." In many ways the Hopi have lived up to the meanings of their name. In fact, to be a Hopi is to strive toward the goals of total reverence and respect for all things and to be at peace with everything by living in accordance with the Creator's instructions.

Is there anything in the Hopi philosophy that we can apply to our lives today? How would the world change if we did so?

PUEBLOS AND KIVAS

The Hopis live in northeast Arizona in villages called pueblos. These pueblos are made of stone and mud, and the buildings in these communities are several stories high.

Beneath the pueblos are underground chambers called *kivas*, which are sacred chambers in which religious ceremonies are held. A fire pit is located in the center of a kiva, and around this centerpiece Hopis would converse, pray, and perform their rituals.

The kiva commemorates the emergence of humanity into the upper world. In each kiva there is a small hole in the floor, which denotes "the umbilical cord" that stems from Mother Earth to humanity.

KACHINAS

Ancestor spirits of the Hopis are known as Kachinas. There are over three hundred of them, and it is believed that they possess great supernatural power. Through ceremonial dances the people ask the Kachinas to send rain. Hopi pottery sometimes depicts a thunderbird (or rain bird), and this relates to their rituals that call for rain.

Kachina Dolls

The Hopis make Kachina dolls, which they give to their daughters and sell to tourists.

Hopi Religion

Hopis believe the world was created by Taiowa (the sun-father) and his nephew, Sotuknang. As time went on, mankind forgot their sun-father and grew corrupt. This caused Sotuknang to destroy the world.

As this destruction took place, a small, faithful group of people was preserved by taking shelter. They emerged from their shelter after the world was restored. The Hopis believe this same scenario was repeated twice before the present world—the fourth world—was created. They also believe it will happen again.[2]

These peaceful people see an interdependent relationship between the upper world (where we live) and the lower world (the realm of the dead). The relationships between day and night and summer and winter are related to this interdependence between the two worlds. They were very familiar with the duality of nature in all its forms.

The Hopis believe that cooperation between the upper and lower realms is absolutely essential in order to maintain the natural cycle of the seasons of the year.

It is interesting to note that Hopi traditional ceremonies are practiced for the benefit of the entire world, not just for their own benefit, almost as a form of intercession for everyone.

Central to the Hopi belief system is the idea that humanity emerged from the Earth, the mother of mankind. The most important religious symbol of the Hopis, therefore, is the Mother Earth symbol.

MOTHER EARTH
SYMBOL

THE DAY OF PURIFICATION

The epigraph at the beginning of this chapter presents the Hopi Blue Star (or Blue Kachina) Prophecy. It is a reference to a future date—a date that is known to them as the Day of Purification.

The blue star is Sirius, and the prophecy states that the Fifth World will emerge when Sirius "... makes its appearance in the heavens." This prophecy may be interpreted either literally or figuratively, but whatever one's interpretation is, it is clear that it is a prediction of monumental change for the entire world.

The Hopis believe they will be preserved when this tumultuous change occurs. Dr. Allen Ross, who has studied Hopi religion and prophecy, believes that World War III is imminent, and he believes it will be a nuclear war that will destroy the United States. When this happens, according to

Dr. Ross, the Hopis will be preserved and many American refugees will flee to Hopi villages for protection.

He writes, "It is only materialistic people who seek to make [bomb] shelters. Those who are at peace in their hearts [the Hopis] already are in the great shelter of life. There is no shelter for evil. Those who take part in the making of world division by ideology are ready to resume life in another world, be they black, white, red, or yellow race. They are all one—brothers."[3]

The Hopi believe that World War III will be a conflict between spiritual and material forces. Spiritual beings will destroy material things, and these spiritual beings will remain in order to create one world and one nation under the one power of the one Creator.

WHEN WILL THE FIFTH WORLD BEGIN?

The Hopi prophecies stem from their oral tradition, which has predicted the coming of the white man, the world wars, and the advent of nuclear weapons. They ultimately state that time will end when humanity emerges into the fifth world. Many believe the transition between the fourth and fifth worlds has already begun.

Some prophecies of the Hopis indicate that time will end in 2012, in full agreement with the Mayan calendar's end date. Their projections even go beyond 2012, by saying that the years after 2012 will be a "golden age" that is filled with peace. However, mankind must go through years of great trial, suffering, and persecution before the time of peace and "one-heartedness" will take place.

WHITE FEATHER'S PROPHECY OF THE LOST WHITE BROTHER

The Rev. David Young, while driving along a desert highway in 1958, stopped to offer a ride to an Indian elder. The minister recorded the words this traveler spoke to him. The message was first published as a mimeographed manuscript that circulated among Methodist and Presbyterian churches during 1959.

"I am White Feather, a Hopi of the ancient Bear Clan. In my long life I have traveled through this land, seeking out my brothers, and learning from them many things full of wisdom. I have followed the sacred paths of my people, who inhabit the forests and many lakes in the east, the land of ice and long nights in the north, and places of holy altars of stone built many years ago by my brothers' fathers in the south. From all these I have heard the stories of the past, and the prophecies of the future. Today, many of the prophecies have turned to stories, and few are left—the past grows longer, and the future grows shorter.

"And now White Feather is dying. His sons have all joined his ancestors, and soon he too shall be with them. But there is no one left, no one to recite and pass on the ancient wisdom. My people have tired of the old ways—the great ceremonies that tell of our origins, of our emergence into the Fourth World, are almost all abandoned, forgotten, yet even this has been foretold. The time grows short.

"My people await Pahana, the lost White Brother [from the stars], as do all our brothers in the land. He will not be like the white men we know now, who are cruel and greedy. We were told of their coming long ago. But still we await Pahana.

"He will bring with him the symbols, and the missing piece of that sacred tablet now kept by the elders, given to him when he left, that shall identify him as our True White Brother.

"The Fourth World shall end soon, and the Fifth World will begin. This the elders everywhere know. The Signs over many years have been fulfilled, and so few are left.

"**This is the First Sign:** We are told of the coming of the white-skinned men, like Pahana, but not living like Pahana, men who took the land that was not theirs. And men who struck their enemies with thunder [interpreted as guns].

"This is the Second Sign: Our lands will see the coming of spinning wheels filled with voices. In his youth, my father saw this prophecy come true with his eyes—the white men bringing their families in wagons across the prairies [interpreted as covered wagons].

"This is the Third Sign: A strange beast like a buffalo but with great long horns will overrun the land in large numbers. These White Feather saw with his eyes—the coming of the white men's cattle [interpreted as longhorn steers].

"This is the Fourth Sign: The land will be crossed by snakes of iron [interpreted as railroad tracks].

"This is the Fifth Sign: The land shall be crisscrossed by a giant spider's web [interpreted as electric-power, telephone, and telegraph lines. This could also be a prophecy of the worldwide web].

"This is the Sixth Sign: The land shall be crisscrossed with rivers of stone that make pictures in the sun [interpreted as highways, with their mirage-producing effects].

"This is the Seventh Sign: You will hear of the sea turning black, and many living things dying because of it [interpreted as oil spills in the oceans].

"This is the Eighth Sign: You will see many youth, who wear their hair long like my people, come and join the tribal nations, to learn their ways and wisdom [interpreted as the hippies].

"This is the Ninth and Last Sign: You will hear of a dwelling-place in the heavens, above the earth, that shall fall with a great crash. It will appear as a blue star. Very soon after this, the ceremonies of my people will cease [interpreted as the U.S. Space Station Skylab, which fell to Earth in 1979. Australian eyewitnesses reported that it was burning blue as it fell].

"These are the signs that great destruction is coming. The world shall rock to and fro. The white man will battle against other people in other lands—with those who possessed the first light of wisdom. There will be many columns of smoke and fire such as White Feather has seen the white man make in the deserts not far from here. [Atomic proving grounds in New Mexico?] Only those which come will cause disease and a great dying.

"Many of my people, understanding the prophecies, shall be safe. Those who stay and live in the places of my people also shall be safe. Then there will be much to rebuild. And soon—very soon afterward—Pahana will return. He shall bring with him the dawn of the Fifth World. He shall plant the seeds of his wisdom in their hearts. Even now the seeds are being planted. These shall smooth the way to the emergence of the Fifth World.

"But White Feather shall not see it. I am old and dying. You—perhaps will see it. In time, in time...."⁴

Has that time come? Are the seeds of preparation being planted in human hearts around the world today?

Many believe that White Feather's conclusion to this prophecy was a vision of a nuclear holocaust that would bring death and destruction to the United States of America.

It is not pleasant to contemplate such a gruesome and frightening scenario, but we all know that it is possible and, indeed, quite plausible. Perhaps White Feather and his predecessors had a source of knowledge that many do not understand and few know how to access. Is this a prediction of what will happen in the United States of America in the very near future? Is there any way to avoid the fulfillment of this prophecy?

THE UNITED NATIONS BUILDING

OTHER HOPI PROPHECIES

One Hopi prophecy warned that mankind should bring nothing back from the moon. This was given well before space travel began, and it apparently anticipated the journey of the Apollo 11 mission that brought samples of lunar soil to Earth. The Hopi warned that this would cause great disturbance to natural laws, resulting in forces being unleashed that would cause massive earthquakes, drastic changes in climate and weather patterns, and widespread social unrest. Is this prophecy being fulfilled in our own time?

In 1959, a six-man delegation of Hopi leaders went to New York City to fulfill a sacred mission in accord with ancient Hopi prophecies. This group, which was led by the spiritual leader Dan Katchongva, went to the United Nations building ("the house of mica") in order to share their wisdom with world leaders ["great leaders from many lands ... gathered to help any people who are in trouble"].

It was believed that a few world leaders from various nations would hear and understand the Hopi warnings and that they would act immediately to right the wrongs that had been done to Native Americans, who believed they had been given permission by the Great Spirit to hold in trust all lands and life for Him.

"IT SHALL BE FULFILLED!"

Their prophecies were not received in the manner they expected, however, for no one [in "the Glass House" — the United Nations] seemed to heed their warnings. Since that time, though, Hopi leaders have returned to the General Assembly of the United Nations with this message: "When the Great Leaders in the Glass House refuse to open the door to you when you stand before it that day, do not be discouraged or turn about on the path you walk, but take courage, determination, and be of great rejoicing in your hearts, for on that day the White Race who are on your land with you have cut themselves from you and thereon lead themselves to the Greatest Punishment at the Day of Purification. Many shall be destroyed for their sins and evil ways. The Great Spirit has decreed it and no one can stop it, change it, or add anything to it. It shall be fulfilled!"

The peace-loving Hopi have given us a great deal to think about in this prophecy and the various messages we have discussed in this chapter. In fact, their overall message paints a grim picture of a definite doomsday, which many of their elders suggest will take place on December 21, 2012.

Tim Hutchinson wrote, "We are a step closer to it now—the doomsday scenario." This doomsday scenario seems very plausible, even likely, in light of the threats of terrorism in our world today.

The holocaust that is predicted by the Hopi Indians could happen very soon due to the proliferation of weapons of mass destruction that are available to so many in our time. What would our world be like if nuclear or biological weapons were unleashed in our major cities?

Jesus said, *"And when ye shall see Jerusalem compassed with armies, then know that the desolation thereof is nigh. Then let them which are in Judaea flee to the mountains ..."* (Luke 21:20-21, KJV).

The Hopi have said that many will flee to their villages in the mesas of Arizona, which they believe will be the only safe place in the end times. Those who do so will be preserved. All others will be destroyed.

Just prior to her death, a Hopi grandmother gave these prophetic words to her grandson: "Make a place for yourself in the mountains because the air will become so hot down here that it will be hard to breathe. And it won't be long."[7]

Is it likely, as Jesus and the Hopi have said, that people will have to run to the mountains in order to survive a possible nuclear devastation? The Hopis truly believe that Doomsday is approaching in the very near future. If they are right, everything is about to change.

This is what Jesus said about that time, *"And as it was in the days of Noah, so shall it be also in the days of the Son of man. They did eat, they drank,... and the flood came, and destroyed them all.... Even thus shall it be in the day when the Son of man is revealed.... Whosoever shall seek to save his life shall lose it; and whosoever shall lose his life shall preserve it. I tell you, in that night there shall be two men in one bed; the one shall be taken, and the other left. Two men shall be in the field; the one shall be taken, and the other left"* (Luke 17:26-36, KJV).

Is this passage describing the end of the world? Are Jesus and the Hopis prophesying about the same event—the Day of Purification, the end of all things? Is that time coming soon? Are there any answers to these questions?

Let us now turn to the prophecies of the Cherokee Nation to see what they have to say about the future.

"Stop acting as if life is a rehearsal. Live this day as if it were your last. The past is over and gone. The future is not guaranteed" (Wayne Dyer).

ENDNOTES

1. *Hopi Prophecies* by Dr. Allen Ross. http://www.crystalinks.com/hopi2.html
2. Ibid.
3. Ibid.
4. *Hopi Civilization.* http://2012wiki.com/index.php?title=Hopi_Civilization
5. *Hopi Prophecies* by Dr. Allen Ross. http://www.crystalinks.com/hopi2.html

6. Ibid.
7. *North American (Hopi) Prophecies* by Lee Brown. http://www.welcomehome.org/rainbow/prophecy/hopi2.html

Other Resources That Were Consulted in the Preparation of This Chapter

1. *Hopi Indians.* http://inkido.indiana.edu/w310work/romac/hopi.htm
2. *Hopi Religion.* http://philtar.ucsm.ac.uk/encyclopedia/nam/hopi.html
3. *Thomas Banyacya, Hopi Elder.* http://www.dreamscape.com/morgana/tethys.htm

Additional Resources You May Wish to Explore

1. *Hopi* by Susanne and Jake Page, Abradale Press, 1994.
2. "Hopi Kachina Tradition: Following the Sun and Moon" by Alph Secakuku, 1995.

6

When the Earth Shakes—the Prophecies of the Cherokees

And in the Year 2012 the Cherokee calendar ends.
And all is reborn. For the Feathered Rattlesnake comes
and shall be seen in the heavens....
CHEROKEE STAR CONSTELLATION—
PROPHECY OF THE RATTLESNAKE[1]

Cherokee prophecies tend to confirm what we have learned about the end times from other indigenous peoples. Beyond this, many predictions of the Cherokee people indicate that a time is coming when time itself will speed up and people will move faster and faster. As a result, parents will no longer have time for their children, and other important parts of life will take a low priority. Has this process already begun?

Are we losing sight of the truth that was stated by Bonnie Friedman: "An unhurried sense of time is in itself a form of wealth"? The Cherokees are very careful to admonish people to slow down when things begin to speed up. This is their advice in anticipation of the fulfillment of their prophecy about the soon-to-come "Third Great Shaking of the Earth."

The Third Great Shaking of the Earth

The first two Great Shakings of the Earth, according to Cherokee teachings, were World War I and World War II.

2012: Is This the End?

The Third Great Shaking might refer to World War III, which the Hopis and others have predicted, or perhaps to a massive, destructive earthquake.

A passage in the Old Testament that was written by the Prophet Joel describes the Day of the Lord (the last days) as follows: *"Blow the trumpet in Zion; sound the alarm on my holy hill. Let all who live in the land tremble, for the day of the Lord is coming. It is close at hand—a day of darkness and gloom, a day of clouds and blackness.... Before them fire devours, behind them a flame blazes.... They rush upon the city; they run along the wall. They climb into the houses; like thieves they enter through the windows. Before them the earth shakes, the sky trembles, the sun and moon are darkened, and the stars no longer shine.... The day of the Lord is great; it is dreadful. Who can endure it?"* (Joel 2:1-11, NIV)

It amazed me when I noted the obvious parallel between this Old Testament prophecy and Cherokee prophecies about the Third Great Shaking of the Earth. Notice how people will be rushing to and fro during the end times, which is what the Cherokees have predicted, as well. Notice, also, that the Bible says that a great shaking of the Earth will take place when the Day of the Lord comes.

The Cherokees believe that this Third Great Shaking of the Earth will occur after the time when human beings learn to live in the "house in the sky"—a possible reference to the space station. Soon thereafter, according to the prophecy, the Great Spirit will grab the Earth with both hands. When this happens, the Earth will undergo a great shaking.

The survivors of this dreadful event, according to Cherokee legend, will become like "hollow shells," because they will be empty within. (Their souls and spirits will lack life and purpose.) Others are described as being like steam—vaporized, if you will. This is a terrible scenario to contemplate, but according to the prophecy, there is hope to consider, as well, for it says that the remnant of survivors will work together to rebuild the circle of the human family.

This, according to the Cherokees, will be followed by peace on Earth.

Can anything be done to prevent this Third Great Shaking of the Earth?

The Cherokee prophets warn, "If we could stop the racial and religious disharmony, we would not have to go through the Third Shaking."

The Bible says, *"At that time his [God's] voice shook the earth, but now he has promised, 'Once more I will shake not only the earth but also the heavens.' The words 'once more' indicate the removing of what can be shaken—that is, created things—so that what cannot be shaken will remain."* (Hebrews 12:26-27, NIV)

Has the Third Great Shaking of the Earth already begun? Remember, the only things that will remain will be those things that cannot be shaken.

THE RATTLESNAKE PROPHECY

The prophecy about the Third Great Shaking of the Earth is a part of the Cherokee prophecies of 1811-1812. These prophecies came about as the result of supernatural visions that were received by individuals.

In 1812, a blazing comet followed by earthquakes gave these prophecies an apocalyptic emphasis. One of these prophecies is known as the Rattlesnake Prophecy, which mentions several significant events related to the year 2012.

The Rattlesnake Prophecy is also known as the Cherokee Star Constellation Prophecy, or the Chickamaugan Prophecy. The latter name comes from the Chickamauga Cherokees who inhabited the southeastern part of the United States.

In this prophecy Quetzalcoatl, the feathered serpent that was mentioned by the Mesoamerican tribes we discussed earlier, emerges once again. The Rattlesnake Prophecy goes on to mention a thirteen-constellation zodiac and other things that take place in the heavens, such as the transit of Venus in 2004 and 2012.[2]

The calendar followed by the Cherokees is based on the Mayan calendar. Hence, its final date is December 21, 2012.

TIME/UNTIME

In the Rattlesnake Prophecy the Cherokees introduce a concept that has come to be known as "Time/Untime." Though this idea is open to interpretation, many believe it serves to contrast western ways of measuring time with the cyclical interpretations of time that have been put forth by the Indians.

Others have interpreted this distinction as pointing to the contrast between the physical and spiritual realms.

The Rattlesnake Prophecy involves a serpent or snake with fifty-two scales upon its mouth. Each of the scales refers to a point on the Cherokee calendar, and, therefore, refers to points on what the Cherokees call the "wheel of time."

By way of these "wheels," the Cherokees were able to make predictions concerning many things about the universe and individuals.

PORTIONS OF THE PROPHECY

The following paragraphs provide us with glimpses into the Rattlesnake Prophecy by way of excerpts that relate to the main theme of this book. I think its predictions will surprise you and cause you to think about the future.

"... when the ages of the rings and wheels tell it is the ending of the age of cycles of five, this will be the sign for the whole earth, for all the earth will see this thing, to wake up from sleep. These fingers that struck Jupiter were the comet fragments that hit Jupiter in the 1990's and the whole earth took of its majesty. This was the sign foretold on the calendar for the Cherokee people to wake up, to come out of sleep.

"The Cherokee calendar also speaks its voice, telling that at this time of the fingers striking Jupiter that Orion Star System will awaken. And the Pleiades [the star system where life originated, according to Cherokee mythology] and Orion will war once again as in old. Jupiter and Venus will awaken to its destiny of Time/Untime of cycles. Orion will war with Pleiades, Jupiter will war with Venus....

"In the year 2004 and 2012 an alignment will take place both on the Cherokee calendar and in the heavens of the Rattlesnake Constellation.... It is the time of the double-headed serpent stick. It is the time of the red of Orion and Jupiter against the white blue of Pleiades and Venus.... It is the time of the Beloved Woman and mysteries of Time/Untime. It is the Time/Untime of the thunderbolt and the spirits of Lightning Mountains.

"In the year 2004 and 2012 the Cherokee Rattlesnake Constellation will take on a different configuration. The Snake itself will remain, however; upon the Rattlesnake shall be added upon its head feathers, its eyes will open and glow, wings spring forth as a winged rattlesnake. It shall have hands and arms and in its hands shall be found a bowl. The bowl will hold blood. Upon its tail of seven rattles shall be the glowing and movement of Pleiades.

"The Rattlesnake shall become a feathered rattlesnake or feathered serpent of Time/Untime. [It is possible that the feathered serpent refers to Quetzalcoatl.]

"And upon the Rattlesnake is also the Milky Way. A crossing of the Milky Way shall be seen at these times.... [2004 and 2012.]

"The Milky Way is also a tree—a stone tree. And upon Stone Tree is as a tree with a tree trunk, branches, a top, and even roots. The flower and the tree is also a tassel as corn.

And upon the flower and the tree is the Tree of Life. Rebirth. Renewal. New.

"And the Cherokee calendar shall end in the year 2012. But upon the times just prior shall be the Feathered Serpent and its prophecy."[3]

The prophecy goes on to describe the writhing of the serpent in the heavens, and by this Cherokees believe that one is able to see into what has been, what is, and what will be. By observing this phenomenon they believe one is able to discern the movement of the "rings of time."

"... And in the year 2004 the Morning Star shall be first and in the year 2012 the Evening Star shall be first. And upon those years the crown of the Feathered Serpent shall bear its colors and honor. The hands shall hold the bowl and the tail shall be as the roots of a Tree. The Pleiades Tree of the beginning...

"And in the year 2012 the Cherokee calendar ends. And all is reborn....

"In the south of the Americas ... it is related as the coming of Quetzalcoatl. The ancient Cherokee relate it as the coming of the Pale One once again."[4]

The prophecy ends on a note of hope and optimism by foretelling the return of Quetzalcoatl—the Pale One. Before he returns, however, the Cherokees prophesy a time of great tribulation, suffering, and hardship.

THE GUARDIANSHIP OF THE EARTH

Another Cherokee prophecy says that the Great Spirit has given the guardianship of the Earth to the red people. The guardianship of the wind was given to the yellow race. The black race was given the guardianship of the water, and the white race was given the guardianship of the fire.[5]

This prophecy goes on to say that the Great Spirit gave each race a set of two stone tablets. It further states that tribes began to send people to the mountains to have visions in order to learn how to survive.

In these supernatural ways, the Cherokees are admonished to remind all people of the sacredness of all things. They teach that this knowledge will bring peace on the Earth. However, the prophecy also warns that if mankind does not learn to honor the sacredness of all things, the Great Spirit will grab the Earth with his hand and shake it violently.[6]

THE GOURD OF ASHES

The world has gone through the First and Second Great Shakings (believed to be World War I and World War II). Now we are on the verge of the Third Great Shaking. This will involve a "gourd of ashes" falling from the air. This "gourd" (believed to represent a nuclear bomb) will make the people like blades of grass in a prairie fire, and things will not grow for many seasons thereafter.

The Cherokee elders referred to the "gourd of ashes" as far back as 1920, and, as time went on, they tried to warn the President of the United States that he should not use such a devastating weapon, because it would have a deleterious effect on the Earth and usher in the Third Great Shaking.

As we know, their words were not heeded. The "gourd of ashes" did, indeed, fall from the sky in Japan and elsewhere. Its effects were immediate, devastating, and long-lasting. In all likelihood, its use in the future will result in nearly total annihilation and destruction.

Long ago, the Cherokees and many other tribes prophesied about a wide variety of future events, which have actually occurred. Some of these are the establishment of the United Nations, space travel, journeys to the moon, the discovery of DNA, genetic splicing, the development of new types of animals, the production of nuclear weapons, and many other things.

The prophecies of the Cherokees were always either-or propositions. This puts the emphasis on our free wills and our power of choice.

In the hope that we will learn to live together in harmony, the Cherokees continue to share their prophetic insights. Ultimately, they explain, the choice is ours.

It's Up to You

A young brave decided he would challenge the aging chief of his tribe. To do so, he captured a little bird and covered it with his hand. Then, in front of several members of the tribe, he asked the chief, "Is the bird I'm holding in my hand alive or dead?"

In posing this question, the boy thought he would embarrass the old man. He reasoned, "If the chief says that the bird is dead, I will simply release it from my hands and prove him wrong. If the chief says the bird is alive, I will simply crush it to death between my hands."

The chief paused, thought carefully, and then said, "It's up to you!"

My study of Cherokee prophecies suggests that how we respond to the warnings will make a big difference in determining their impact upon our lives. We do have some power of choice about these matters. Will we choose to be fearful and let things happen to us? Or will we be calm and proactive, taking action to do what we can to make the world a better place?

What truths can we take from the Cherokee prophecies?

How much choice do we actually have with regard to these warnings?

There is a time for everything,
And a season for every activity under heaven:
A time to be born and a time to die,

A time to plant and a time to uproot,
A time to kill and a time to heal,
A time to break down and a time to build,
A time to weep and a time to laugh,
A time to mourn and a time to dance,
A time to scatter stones and a time to gather them;
A time to embrace and a time to refrain,
A time to search and a time to give up,
A time to keep and a time to throw away,
A time to tear and a time to mend,
A time to be silent and a time to speak,
A time to love and a time to hate,
A time for war and a time for peace....

*He has made everything beautiful in its time. He has also
set eternity in the hearts of men; yet they cannot fathom what
God has done from beginning to end.... I know that everything
God does will endure forever; nothing can be added to it and
nothing taken from it. God does it so that men will revere him.
Whatever is has already been, and what will be has been before;
and God will call the past into account.... God will bring to
judgment both the righteous and the wicked, for there will be
a time for every activity, a time for every deed* (Ecclesiastes
3:1-8, NIV).

ENDNOTES

1. *When the Earth Shakes: the Cherokee Prophecies of 1811-12.*
   http://findarticles.com/p/articles/mi_hb3459/is_199306/ai_
   n8235230/pg_1

2. *Cherokee Prophecies.* http://www.think-aboutit.com/native/
   CherokeeProphecies.htm

3. Ibid.

4. Ibid.

5. *First People—the Legends.* http://www.firstpeople.us/FP-Html-Legends/Cherokee_Prophecies-Cherokee.html

6. *Cherokee Prophecies.* http://www.think-aboutit.com/native/CherokeeProphecies.htm

Other Resources That Were Consulted in the Preparation of This Chapter

1. *Cherokee Prophecies.* http://www.crystalinks.com/cherokee.html

2. *Cherokee Civilization.* http://2012wiki.com/index.php?title=Cherokee_civilization

Additional Resources You May Wish to Explore

1. *"Cherokee Healing: Myth, Dreams, and Medicine"* by L. Irwin. American Indian Quarterly, Volume 16, 1992.

2. *"Blood Politics, Racial Classification, and Cherokee National Identity: the Trials and Tribulations of the Cherokee Freedmen"* by Circe Sturm. American Indian Quarterly, Volume 22, 1998.

7

The Prognostications of Merlin the Magician, Mother Shipton, and Nostradamus

Luxury shall overspread the land, and fornication shall not
cease to debauch mankind. Famine shall then return, and the
inhabitants shall grieve for the destruction of their cities.
In those days the oaks of the forests shall burn, and acorns
grow upon lime trees! The Severn sea shall discharge itself
through seven mouths, and the river Usk burn for seven
months! Fishes shall die in the heat thereof,
and from them serpents will be born.
MERLIN THE MAGICIAN[1]

For those who live the century through
In fear and trembling this shall do.
Flee to the mountains and the dens
To bog and forest and wild fens.
For storms will rage and oceans roar
When Gabriel stands on sea and shore,
And as he blows his wondrous horn
Old worlds die and new be born.
ATTRIBUTED TO MOTHER SHIPTON[2]

The year of the great seventh number accomplished,
It will appear at the time of the games of slaughter:
Not far from the great millennial age,
When the buried will go out from their tombs.
NOSTRADAMUS[3]

A Myth Is a Metaphor

As the late mythologist Joseph Campbell said, "A myth is a metaphor." Most myths are not meant to be taken literally. In fact, a metaphor is a figurative comparison between two entities. Figurative language is never meant to be taken literally; rather, it is symbolic in nature. Its purpose is to paint a verbal picture—an image that helps us to grasp something that is abstract.

The myths of ancient people are meant to convey spiritual truths and realities that are perceived by a given culture. Hence, when a Mayan talks about a "sacred tree," he is using a metaphor to help us understand a spiritual truth by comparing it to a physical reality. The same would be true of the Cherokees' "gourd of ashes." Not a literal tree and not a literal gourd.

Ancient prophecies are often built from metaphorical myths, which endeavor to bridge the gap between the spiritual realm and the physical world. When David wrote, "The Lord is my shepherd," for example, he was conveying spiritual truth via metaphors, and in this one sentence we find at least three metaphors. Two are direct and one is implied.

First, when he uses the word "Lord" to describe God, he is revealing several attributes about God: He is a Ruler, a leader, and a member of royalty. When he says, "… my shepherd," he is telling us that God takes care of us in the same way a shepherd cares for his sheep. This opens the door to several understandings and interpretations: God provides for us, He leads us, He protects us, etc.

There is an implied metaphor here, as well. If the Lord is our Shepherd, then we are simply sheep. What does this say about our intelligence, our neediness, our weakness, etc?

In the same way myths, prophecies, and legends are open to a variety of interpretations. In our attempts to understand and interpret them, we can gain important spiritual insights and understandings, whether the prophecy is to be taken literally or figuratively.

In the Cherokee prophecy of the Great Spirit holding the Earth in His hands and shaking it, we learn many things, but these things are not necessarily meant to be taken literally. Does a spirit have hands? To take it a step further, does a spirit even need hands? The answer to both questions is obviously no. However, this idea paints a verbal picture for us, one that is clear, easy to see, and easy to understand.

The wizard Merlin and the seer Mother Shipton are legendary figures, a mixture of truth and reality. Both individuals actually existed, but what we know about them is limited and much may have been added to their writings, biographies, and statements.

Their prophecies call for intensive study and interpretation, because they are filled with metaphors and other figures of speech. The same can be said for the quatrains of Nostradamus, who was an actual historical figure. The words of all three of these soothsayers have been interpreted in a variety of ways.

Let's now take a look at their predictions in an effort to learn what they had to say, if anything, about the end times.

MERLIN THE MAGICIAN

Most of us have heard of Merlin the Magician in connection with the medieval legends surrounding King Arthur and the Knights of the Round Table. He is frequently portrayed as a thin, old man with a white beard—a wise wizard who wore a pointed hat.

Merlin and King Arthur from
Idylls of the Kings.

Was Merlin a real man or a strictly legendary figure, or was he a combination of truth and fantasy? It is likely that he was a blend of at least two individuals: Myrddin Wyllt (Merlinus Caldeonensis), a Welsh bard and prophet who went insane as a result of witnessing the horrors of war, and Aurelius Ambrosius, a figure from the writings of Nennius (*Historia Brittonum—History of Britain*) in the ninth century. It is reported that Myrddin Wyllt fled civilization to become a feral man of the forest during the sixth century.

It is believed that Aurelius Ambrosius (aka Ambrosius Aurelianus), on the other hand, was an actual historical war leader, but it is also likely that the events of his life were greatly embellished by Nennius in an effort to give this figure an aura of heroism beyond what might have actually been true.

For example, Nennius said that Ambrosius did not have a human father. In fact, the traditional biography of Merlin said that he was the son of an incubus (a demonic spirit) and a mortal woman.

Much of what we know about Merlin was created by Geoffrey of Monmouth, who wrote *Prophetiae Merlini* (*The Prophecies of Merlin*), *Historia Regum Britanniae* (*The History of the Kings of Britain*) in the twelfth century (a few hundred years after Nennius wrote), and *Vita Merlini*. His description of Merlin and his supernatural abilities was immediately popular in England.

Geoffrey's portrayal of Merlin is in all probability an amalgamation of both Myrddin Wyllt (Merlinus Caledonensis) and Ambrosius Aurelianus, as was noted above. He gave this name to the man he wrote about: Merlin Ambrosius—an obvious composite of the two different men.[4]

According to legend, Merlin "engineered" the birth of King Arthur through his magical powers. After Arthur became king, Merlin became one of his most important advisors. Later, however, according to the legend, he was bewitched and imprisoned by the Lady of the Lake.

Merlin (aka Marlin) was known as an ancient oracle of doom, and he was considered to be one of Europe's greatest seers and soothsayers.

It is said that this remarkable man prophesied about terrorist attacks, global warming, and planetary catastrophes that have happened and may well continue to happen during the times in which we live.

Certainly the rise of terrorism all over the world is in the daily news. Likewise, global warming has become one of the dominant issues of our times. Hundreds of years before anyone knew or thought about America, Merlin predicted the emergence of an unknown country across the sea by name (Armorica).[5]

He also foretold that the British would be victorious over Napoleon at Vanlo, and he foresaw the Nazi Holocaust.

Let's take a brief look at what he had to say about the twentieth and twenty-first centuries. First, it is reported that he foresees a major disaster taking place in Great Britain. Was this the bombing of London, or is it some future terrorist attack?

The days after this British event, according to Merlin, will grow increasingly darker for the entire globe. He says that the world will end in a terrible apocalypse. He seems to predict that a great polar shift will occur, and this will cause great upheaval on Planet Earth. Unlike the Mayans, however, Merlin does not provide us with specific dates.

Merlin predicted that the planets in our solar system will "run riot" through the constellations, completely off their normal paths of rotation. This could well lead to a polar shift. Merlin also foresaw "talking stones," and it is true that the stone—the quartz stone, in particular—is the basis of much of modern technology. Quartz is used in cell phones and computers, and silicone quartz stores information.

Here are some of Merlin's prophecies that were recorded by Geoffrey of Monmouth and others. Remember that these predictions demand a great deal of interpretation, for they are metaphorical in nature:

"The seas shall rise up in the twinkling of an eye, and the dust of the ancients shall be destroyed." [Modern science seems to confirm this prediction by saying that the coastlines of the world will recede by as much as five feet during this century due to global warming. Likewise, tsunamis are expected to increase in both frequency and destructive power.][6]

"The cult of religion shall be destroyed completely, and the ruin of the churches shall be clear for all to see. The race that is oppressed shall prevail in the end, for it will resist the savagery of the invaders." [Certainly communism in the Soviet Union and China has attempted to fulfill this prophecy without complete success through the atheistic persecution of the Church. The context of this prophecy makes it seem possible or even likely that Merlin was referring to Christians as being "the race that is oppressed." Or was he referring to a particular race of people, such as Native Americans, Tibetans, black people, etc?][7]

"Death will lay hold of the people and destroy all the nations. Those who are left alive will abandon their native soil and will sow their seeds in the fields of others." [This statement is a clear pronouncement of doomsday.][8]

"The mountains of Armorica [interpreted as America] shall erupt." [Volcanic activity in the United States has been minimal in recent years (except in Washington and Alaska), but other natural disasters have done horrendous damage. Many believe that a massive volcano will arise and erupt within Yellowstone National Park in the very near future.][9]

"The father shall not know his own son, for human beings will copulate wantonly as cattle do." [This prophecy is being fulfilled throughout the world.][10]

"Men will become drunk with the wine which is offered to them; they will turn their backs on Heaven and fix their eyes on the Earth." [Heaven means little to many people today,

MOTHER SHIPTON

because they have fixed their eyes on the things of Earth and in the process many have become addicted to alcohol and drugs. So many have lost any concept of sin and the fear of God.][11]

"The harvests will dry up through the stars' anger, and all moisture from the sky will cease." [A prophecy of drought and famine that could result from global warming and other natural phenomena.][12]

"Before the amber glow of Mercury the bright light of the Sun shall grow dim, and this will strike horror into those who witness it."[13] [About the end times, Jesus said, *"And great earthquakes shall be in divers places, and famines, and pestilences; and fearful sights and great signs shall there be from heaven.... And there shall be signs in the sun, and in the moon, and in the stars; and upon the earth distress of nations, with perplexity; the sea and the waves roaring"* (Luke 21:11-25, KJV, emphasis mine).

These words of Merlin give us much to think about and contemplate in our present day even though they were first recorded during the early Middle Ages.

The late medieval period and early Renaissance brought forth another prophet named Mother Shipton. Let's now take a look at what she had to say about the future.

MOTHER SHIPTON (1488-1561)

Years later (in the early 1500's) a lady from Yorkshire, England, Mother Shipton (aka Ursula Sontheil), began to prophesy. Her prophecies were both specific and direct. For example, she accurately predicted the death of King Henry VIII, the defeat of the Spanish Armada, the Great Plague of London, and the Great Fire of London.[14]

It is likely that Mother Shipton was an actual historical figure, but some of her prophecies might have been composed after her death by others. No matter who wrote them, these prophecies seem to be uncannily accurate and very intriguing.

The first publication of Mother Shipton's prophecies took place in 1641, less than one hundred years after her death. The book was written in the form of a diary, the recollections of Joanne Waller, a woman who served as a maid in Mother Shipton's household.

A better organized and well-edited version of the prophecies was published in 1684. The latter book describes Mother Shipton as being hideously ugly. Despite her appearance, though, she spent her life telling fortunes and making predictions.

Mother Shipton's most famous prophecy is known as the "End-of-the-World Prophecy." In this prognostication Ursula Southeil predicts an era of global progress that will be followed by chaos and devastation. This prophecy echoes the predictions of the Mayans, the *I Ching*, and Merlin the Magician.

Here are some of the prophetic verses that are attributed to Mother Shipton:

> *A house of glass shall come to pass*
> *In England. But alas, alas*
> *A war will follow with the work*
> *Where dwells the Pagan and the Turk.*
> *These states will lock in fiercest strife*
> *And seek to take each other's life.*

[Mother Shipton is prophesying about a war that will involve Middle Eastern peoples and nations—"… the Pagan and the Turk." A highly placed U.S. Intelligence official foresees this, as well. In an article dated March 10, 2009, this official states that a coming war will have Israel as its epicenter.][15]

> *When North shall thus divide the South*
> *And eagle build in lion's mouth*
> *Then tax and blood and cruel war*

Shall come to every humble door....
Then love shall die and marriage cease
And nations wane as babes decrease.
And wives shall fondle cats and dogs
And men live much the same as hogs....
For then shall mighty wars be planned
And fire and sword shall sweep the land.
When pictures seem alive with movements free [motion
pictures?]
When boats like fishes swim beneath the sea, [submarines?]
When men like birds shall scour the sky [airplanes?]
Then half the world, deep drenched in blood shall die....
Flee to the mountains and the dens
To bog and forest and wild fens.
For storms will rage and oceans roar
When Gabriel stands on sea and shore
And as he blows his wondrous horn
Old worlds die and new be born....

[This part of Mother Shipton's prophecy rings with biblical
authority. The Apostle Paul wrote, *"For the Lord himself will
come down from heaven, with a loud command, with the voice
of the archangel and with the trumpet call of God, and the
dead in Christ will rise first"* (1 Thessalonians 4:16, NIV).]

For seven days and seven nights
Man will watch this awesome sight.
The tides will rise beyond their ken
To bite away the shores and then

[Here, Mother Shipton is prophesying about natural
calamities that may be caused by global warming and
other environmental factors. Science seems to confirm this
prophecy through recent predictions given by geologists and
oceanographers.]

The mountains will begin to roar
And earthquakes split the plain to shore.
And flooding waters, rushing in
Will flood the lands with such a din
[Volcanic activity, earthquakes, tsunamis, and floods—a repeated scenario in many prophecies about the end times.]

That mankind cowers in muddy fen
And snarls about his fellow men
He bares his teeth and fights and kills
And secrets food in secret hills
And ugly in his fear, he lies
To kill marauders, thieves and spies.

[A recent prophecy by the Rev. David Wilkerson, author of *The Cross and the Switchblade* and founder of Teen Challenge and Times Square Church in New York City, paints a similar picture. Wilkerson prophesies, "An earth-shattering calamity is about to happen. It is going to be so frightening, we are all going to tremble—even the godliest among us. It will engulf the whole megaplex, including areas of New Jersey and Connecticut. Major cities all across America will experience riots and blazing fires—such as we saw in Watts, Los Angeles, years ago. There will be riots and fires in cities worldwide. There will be looting.... We are under God's wrath." Wilkerson urges everyone to stockpile a thirty-day supply of food and other necessities to deal with the catastrophe he says he has foreseen.[16] Mother Shipton said, "... and secrets food in secret hills, and ugly in fears he lies, to kill marauders, thieves, and spies."]

Man flees in terror from the floods
And kills, and rapes and lies in blood
And spilling blood by mankind's hands
Will stain and bitter many lands....

Man forgets, and smiles, and carries on
To apply himself—too late, too late
For mankind has earned deserved fate....
[Is this the wrath of God that David Wilkerson, the Bible,
and so many others warn us about?]

But slowly they are routed out
To seek diminishing water spout
And men will die of thirst before
The oceans rise to mount the shore.
And lands will crack and rend anew
You think it strange. It will come true.
And in some far off distant land
Some men—oh, such a tiny band
Will have to leave their solid mount
And span the earth, those few to count,
Who survives this ... and then
Begin the human race again.[17]

There are many commonalities between Mother Shipton's
predictions and some of the prophecies we've already studied.
Essentially, she says that the end times will be filled with
natural disasters, war, death, and destruction. However, after
all the chaos and destruction have passed, the human race will
have a new beginning.

Like some of the ancient prophets, she suggests that
after the Earth passes through this cycle and is cleansed of
corruption, the planet will be renewed and mankind will begin
all over again. This is very similar to the Mayan speculations
about the five eras the world must pass through.

Now, let's move ahead a few years and examine the
predictions of a French astrologer named Michel de
Nostredame (Nostradamus).

Nostradamus

NOSTRADAMUS (1503-1566)

An astrologer is a person who endeavors to see into the future by studying what he or she believes to be the effects of the sun, the moon, and the stars upon human life and behavior. Nostradamus was a physician who spent the latter part of his life in pursuit of knowledge about the future based on what he observed in the heavens. He wrote down his findings in the form of poetic quatrains (942 in all) that were published in a book entitled *Centuries*. He is, perhaps, the most famous of all the "doomsday prophets." In fact, his nickname has become "The Prophet of Doom."[18]

As a physician, Nostradamus treated many people who suffered from the Bubonic Plague. Ironically, he lost the members of his own family to the same disease. This terrible experience may have led him to seek answers through divination. He would write lengthy letters to world leaders in an effort to warn them about future events.

Because soothsaying and magic were banned by the Roman Catholic Church and Nostradamus lived during the time of the Spanish Inquisition, which called for capital punishment for those who engaged in fortune-telling and similar practices, Nostradamus was forced to "hide" many of his messages by scrambling them and giving them an esoteric quality. The quatrains are not written in chronological order, and this makes it more difficult to discern what eras he is referring to. Another complicating factor is that the quatrains were written in French, with some Italian, Greek, and Latin thrown in to confuse the authorities. As a result, their translation into English may be flawed in places.

Though his quatrains are open to different interpretations, the followers of Nostradamus say that he predicted the French Revolution, Hitler's birth and rise to power, the assassination of President John F. Kennedy, the Great Fire of London, and the exile of Napoleon.

The prediction of the death of King Henry II as the result of a jousting accident was one of Nostradamus's first fulfilled prophecies:

The young lion will overcome the older one,
On the field of combat in a single battle;
He will pierce his eyes through a golden cage,
Two wounds made one, then he dies a cruel death.[19]

Even though Nostradamus had warned the king that this would happen, the monarch ignored him and entered a jousting competition with a younger man, the Comte de Montgomery. During the final bout of this jousting event, Montgomery's lance shattered, and two large splinters penetrated the king's gilded visor ("a golden cage"). One splinter went through his eye, and the other drove deeply into the king's temple. Both splinters penetrated his brain. Henry lived in painful agony for ten days ("a cruel death"), then expired, as Nostradamus had prophesied.

Regarding recent events in history, his followers say that Nostradamus revealed the destruction of the space shuttle Challenger, the death of Princess Diana, and the destruction of the World Trade Center on September 11, 2001.

Here is what Nostradamus wrote that is interpreted as a prophecy of 9/11:

In the year 1999, in the seventh month,
From the sky will come the great king of terror,
Bringing back to life the great king of the Mongols.
Before and after, Mars to reign by good fortune.[20]

This is a particularly interesting prophecy that could possibly refer to the catastrophe that took place on September 11, 2001. Note that the terror will come from the sky. However, the date is wrong. To account for this, the followers of Nostradamus explain that he often wrote in anagrams.

Therefore, the date of 1999 may not be anything more than a numeric anagram.

Some believe that the prophet is referring to the anti-Christ when he says, "... will come the great King of Terror."[21] This is an interesting interpretation, and the word "terror" is particularly poignant for our present times. Is there a connection between Islamic terrorism and the anti-Christ?

In another quatrain Nostradamus mentions, "Earth-shaking fire from the center of the Earth will cause the towers around the New City to shake." Is this a possible reference to 9/11, as well—"... the towers around the New City ..."?[22]

Incidentally, David Wilkerson, the preacher we referred to before, prophesied about the events of 9/11 six weeks before they took place. As a result, he and the members of his church spent those weeks in prayer.

The central purpose of Nostradamus's writing appears to be to warn us about the coming Apocalypse:

The sloping park, great calamity,
Through the lands of the West and Lombardy
The fire in the ship, plague and captivity;
Mercury in Sagittarius, Saturn fading.

What does this quatrain mean? (It comes from *Century 10, Quatrain 79.*) Lombardy, in all likelihood, refers to Italy and Europe, whereas "the lands of the West" may well be a reference to North and South America. There seems to be general agreement that Nostradamus is predicting massive earthquakes in both hemispheres to take place right before the end of the world.

Nostradamus's astrological references to the heavenly bodies of Mercury, Sagittarius, and Saturn are open to wide and varied interpretation. His field is the pseudo-science of astrology, not the science of astronomy, so it is impossible to get precise dates for what he is foreseeing here.

OTHER SIGNIFICANT QUOTES FROM NOSTRADAMUS

The following quotations about the future have been adapted from the writings of Nostradamus:

"The dreadful war which is prepared in the West, the following year the pestilence will come, so very dreadful that young nor old nor animal [will survive]." [A possible reference to World War III or the Battle of Armageddon?][23]

Regarding the Return of Jesus Christ, Nostradamus writes, "This will be preceded by an eclipse of the sun, more obscure and tenebrose [dark and gloomy] than has ever been seen since the creation of the world, except that [eclipse] after the death and passion of Jesus Christ."[24]

Regarding the anti-Christ and his time on Earth, Nostradamus declares, "The third anti-Christ [some say that Napoleon was the first anti-Christ and Hitler was the second. Who will the third one be? Is he already on the planet?] soon annihilates everything, twenty-seven years of blood his war will last. The unbelievers dead, captives, exiled with blood, human bodies, water and red hail covering the Earth."[25]

Here is another statement by Nostradamus about the anti-Christ: "The anti-Christ returns for the last time. All the Christian and infidel nations will tremble for the space of twenty-five years. Wars and battles will be more grievous than ever. Towns, cities, and all other structures will be destroyed. ... So many evils by Satan's prince will be committed that almost the entire world will find itself undone and desolated. Before these events, many rare birds will cry in the air, 'Now! Now!' and sometime later will vanish."[26]

[The climate of the times in which Nostradamus wrote caused him to use codes and riddles to cover some of his true meanings. Many believe that the birds he refers to here are actually human beings who are visionaries and will endeavor to alert the citizens of the world to the coming dangers, so that they might be able to take steps to avert them.]

Nowhere does Nostradamus mention the year 2012, but there is evidence to suggest that many of his futuristic statements could well refer to the times in which we live.

A list of the Seven Signs that will precede the end has been compiled from various sources, including Nostradamus and the holy Bible, as follows:

1. The three major religions of the world will decline.

2. There will be riots, turmoil, revolutions, and bloodshed all over the world.

3. Jesus said that there would be wars and rumors of war.

4. Famines, droughts, floods, and other natural disasters.

5. Air and water pollution.

6. Earthquakes. (Many predict that the Big One will occur in the very near future, and some seismologists suggest that it will take place in the Midwestern United States rather than in California, though, as I write, swarming—a precursor of earthquakes—is taking place in southern California.)

7. Plagues, pestilence, and rampant disease.

Many of these signs are already in effect, and some have already occurred. Will 2012 be the climax of human history as we know it?

Lawrence E. Joseph writes, "The year 2012 has the mark of destiny upon it. Judging from the facts gathered for this book [*Apocalypse 2012*], there is at least an even chance of some massive tragedy and/or great awakening occurring or commencing in that year. The question ultimately is not if but when, not so much the exact date as whether or not this transformational event will occur within our own or our loved ones' lifetime. The value of the 2012 deadline is that, being so close, it forces us to confront the myriad possibilities for global catastrophe, to gauge their likelihood and destructive potential, and to examine how prepared we are to respond to them, individually and as a civilization."[27]

Endnotes

1. *Merlin—Merlin's Prophecies.* http://www.crystalinks.com/merlin.html
2. *Mother Shipton Prophecies.* http://www.nostradamus-repository.org/shipton.html
3. *Nostradamus.* http://www.2012endofdays.org/more/Nostradamus.php
4. *Merlin—Merlin's Propheices.* http://www.crystalinks.com/merlin.html
5. Ibid.
6. Ibid.
7. Ibid.
8. Ibid.
9. *Prophecies of Merlin the Magician.* http://www.wovoca.com/prophecy-merlin-the-magician.htm
10. *Merlin—Merlin's Prophecies.* http://www.crystalinks.com/merlin.html
11. Ibid.
12. Ibid.
13. Ibid.
14. *Mother Shipton's Prophecies.* http://www.crystalinks.com/shipton.html
15. *Mother Shipton Prophecies.* http://www.nostradamus-repository.org/shipton.html
16. *Trend Predictors—Earth-shattering Calamity About to Happen.* David Wilkerson. WorldNetDaily, 2009.
17. *Prophecies of Mother Shipton.* http://www.museumofhoaxes.com/hoax/Hoaxipedia/Prophecies_of_Mother_Shipton/
18. *Who Was Nostradamus?* http://www.nostradamus101.com/prophecies/part1/
19. *Famous Fulfilled Prophecies of Nostradamus.* http://www.nostradamus101.com/prophecies/part2/

20. *Nostradamus and the Present Day.* http://www.
nostradamus101.com/prophecies/part3/
21. Ibid.
22. Ibid.
23. *Nostradamus.* http://www.geocities.com/timongarretson/
oldschool/nostradamus.html?200911
24. Ibid.
25. Ibid.
26. Ibid.
27. Joseph, Lawrence E. *Apocalypse 2012.* Broadway Books, New
York, 2007.

Other Resources That Were Consulted in the Preparation of This Chapter

1. http://techgle.blogspot.com/2008/09/doomsday-2012-
december-21-full-overview_29.html
2. *Merlin.* http://en.wikipedia.org/wiki/Merlin
3. *Merlin the Wizard.* http://www.castles.me.uk/merlin-the-
wizard.htm
4. *Ursula Southeil.* http://en.wikipedia.org/wiki/Ursula_Southeil
5. *The Facts About Nostradamus and His Prophecies* by Dan
Corner. http://www.evangelicaloutreach.org/nostradamus.htm

Additional Resources You May Wish to Explore

1. *The New Arthurian Encyclopedia* by Norris J. Lacy. Published
by Garland, New York, 1991.
2. *Celtic Myth and Arthurian Romance* by Roger Sherman
Loomis. Columbia University Press, New York, 1927.

THE LAST-POPE PROPHECY AND OTHER ROMAN CATHOLIC PROPHECIES

In the final persecution of the Holy Roman Church there will reign Petrus Romanus, who will feed his flock amid many tribulations; and when these things are finished, the seven-hilled city [Rome] will be destroyed, and the dreadful Judge will judge the people.
SAINT MALACHY[1]

IS THE END OF THE WORLD IMMINENT?

This chapter deals with certain prophecies that are attributed to the Virgin Mary, various saints of the church, Jesus Christ, and an Irish-Catholic archbishop, who became the first Irish saint (Saint Malachy—1094-1148). Though the Roman Catholic Church has been very cautious and careful about accepting many prophecies and visions as being true, there are certain prophetic pronouncements, such as Saint Malachy's and those surrounding apparitions of the Virgin Mary, that have found great acceptance among many Catholics and their leaders. This chapter discusses a few of these and presents excerpts from the prophecies themselves.

Prophecies, miracles, visions, and apparitions are evaluated by the church in an effort to determine their authenticity and reliability. Whenever possible, these supernatural phenomena

THE VIRGIN MARY

are documented with evidence from science, eyewitnesses, and other sources.

There were more than three hundred reported apparitions of Mary during the twentieth century alone. Often, according to witnesses, these visitations are accompanied with displays of thunder and lightning, unusual clouds, and angels. Many of these events also include intriguing prophecies about the future.

Therefore, before we take a look at the Last-pope Prophecy that was put forth by Saint Malachy, let's investigate some of the other prophecies that have circulated among Catholics through the centuries. What, if anything, do they have to say about the end times? Do any of their prophetic words agree with the prophecies we've already studied?

Please note that it is rare to find specific dates mentioned in these prophecies.

Our Lady of La Salette

An apparition of the Virgin Mary was reported by two
young girls in La Salette, France. It was reported to have
occurred on September 19, 1846. Maxime Giraud (aged
eleven) and Melanie Calvat (aged fourteen) were approaching
a mountain stream when they saw what they described as a
ball of light.

The girls said "... a beautiful lady, all light and flowers ..."
emerged from the radiance. She sat crying on a large rock
near the river and began prophesying: "France, Italy, Spain
and England will be at war. Blood will flow on the streets,
Frenchmen will fight Frenchmen and Italian against Italian
and in the end will come a war that will be terrible.

"For a period of time God will not remember Italy or
France, for they will have forgotten the Gospel. The evil ones
will display all their malice and there will be murders even in
houses. At the first blow of the sword of God which will fall,
like lightning on humanity, the mountains and all nature will
tremble because the disorder and the misdeeds of man will rise
to the vault of heaven.

"Paris will be destroyed by fire and Marseilles will be
inundated by the sea. Other great cities will be destroyed by
fire and razed to the ground. The just will have to suffer much.
... There will be reconciliation between God and man and
peace.... But this peace will not last for long ... and the sins of
men will be the cause of all the punishment which will once
again be meted out to Earth.

"A forerunner of anti-Christ will marshal an army drawn
from all nations, united under his banner. He will lead them
in a bloody war against those still faithful to the living God.
He will shed much blood.... Then there will be seen many
types of punishment on Earth besides the diseases and hunger
which will be universal. Wars will follow wars and the final
one will be led by one of the ten kings of anti-Christ, who

2012: IS THIS THE END?

will have only one will and will be the only ones to rule in the world....

"For the evil done by men, even nature, will cry out and earthquakes will occur in protest even against those who have committed crimes on Earth. The Earth will tremble and you yourself will also tremble.... Tremble! The Lord is on the point of giving you into the hands of your enemies, inasmuch as the holy places are contaminated by corruption. Many convents are no longer houses of God, but pastures of 'Asmodeus,' that is of the devil, impurity, and their followers.

"Thus the time will be reached in which the anti-Christ will be born of a Jewish nun, a false virgin, who will have intimate relations with the ancient serpent, the master of luxury. His father will be a bishop. As soon as he is born, he will have teeth and pronounce blasphemies; in a word, he will be a born devil....

"The seasons will change their characteristics, the Earth will be lit with a fiendish red light; the water and the fire will cause terrible seismic movements which will engulf mountains and cities.

"Rome will lose the Faith and become the seat of the anti-Christ. The demons allied to anti-Christ will operate on Earth and in the sky and humanity will become worse. But God will not give up His truly faithful servants, who are men of goodwill. The gospel will be preached everywhere to all the people and the nations will know the truth....

"I make an urgent appeal to the whole universe. I call the true disciples of God, who lives and reigns in the sky! I use my voice as the perfect imitator of the Word Incarnate, Christ, the only Savior of men....

"Woe to the inhabitants of the Earth. There will be sanguinary war, hunger, pestilence and epidemics, terrible rains of insects, thunder which will shake entire cities, earthquakes, which will make entire regions uninhabitable. Voices will be heard in the air, and men will strike their heads against the wall, wishing for death, but this will bring them, for their part, terrible torture. Blood will flow everywhere. Who could ever report victory unless God shortened the time of trial?

"The time is at hand. The abyss is opening; the king of darkness is watching, the beast is watching with his subjects, who will proclaim him 'savior of the world.' He will rise into the air superbly to reach the sky, but the breath of Archangel Michael will kill him. He will fall back and the Earth will shake without ceasing for three days. It will then open its womb full of fire and the beast and his followers will be allowed into the eternal abyss of inferno. Then water and fire will purify the Earth to destroy all human pride and everything will be renewed."[2]

According to this prophecy, the end times will be an era of upheaval all over the Earth. There will be earthquakes, floods, pestilence, disease, war, disobedience, and great suffering. This description is an echo of earlier prophecies, and it gives us a glimpse into certain aspects of Christian eschatology, particularly with regard to the anti-Christ, that we will examine more thoroughly in a later chapter.

As you read, you will note that many of these Catholic prophecies predict massive catastrophes that stem from climatic and geological changes.

Here again, we have a prophecy that predicts renewal after massive destruction, so this prophecy, like several earlier ones, ends on a positive note.

SAINT JOHN BOSCO

John Bosco (aka Giovanni Bosco)—1815-1888—is the patron saint of editors and homeless children. He founded the religious order of the Salesians (the Society of Saint Francis de Sales). Saint John Bosco spent his life working with homeless children. He was also devoted to the Virgin Mary, and he said that he received prophecies from her.

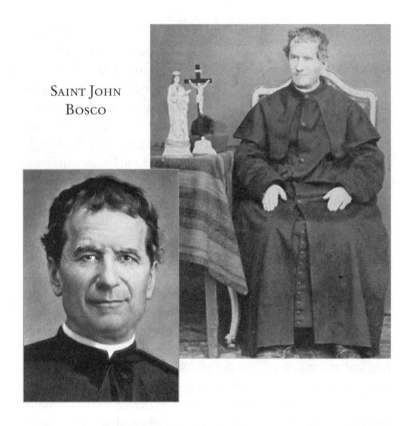

Saint John
Bosco

One of those prophecies declares that the Roman Catholic Church and the papacy will be forced to leave Rome when "Cossack horses will drink from St. Peter's fountain."[3] [Are "Cossack horses" a reference to Russia?]

The most famous of the prophecies recorded by Saint John Bosco has many implications for the end times: "War comes from the south, peace from the north. French laws no longer recognize the Creator, but the Creator will make himself recognized and will visit her thrice with the rod of His wrath....

"Ah, but you, Italy, land of blessings! Who has steeped you in desolation? Blame not your enemies, but rather your friends. Can you not hear your children asking for the bread of faith and finding only those who smash it to pieces? [This sentence has profound implications and applications related to the clergy sexual abuse scandal of our present day.] What shall I do? I shall strike the shepherds, I shall disperse the flock, until those sitting on the throne of Moses search for good pastures and the flock listens attentively and is fed.

"Of the flock and over the shepherds My hand will weigh heavy. Famine, pestilence, and war will be such that mothers will have to cry on account of the blood of their sons and of their martyrs dead in a hostile country.

"And to you, Rome, what will happen? Ungrateful Rome, effeminate Rome, proud Rome! You have reached such a height that you search no further. You admire nothing else in your Sovereign except luxury, forgetting that you and your glory stand upon Golgotha....

"Rome! To you I will come four times....

"There will come a violent hurricane. Iniquity is consummated. Sin will have its end....

"It was a dark night. Men could no longer tell which way to take in order to return to their homes....

"And then there came a furious storm....

"Instantly two angels were seen carrying a banner; ... they said, '... Go quickly and console your children. Write your brothers dispersed throughout the world that there must be a reform in the morals of men. That cannot be obtained except by distributing to the people the bread of the Divine Word. Catechize the children, preach the detaching of the heart from the things of the Earth. The time has come....'"[4]

The words of this prophecy, as they were recorded by Saint John Bosco, put the emphasis upon people turning from their wicked ways, teaching their children about the Lord, and serving God and humanity. It seems as if he is saying that, if we will change our ways, some of the calamities he predicted may be averted. It is interesting to note that much of this prophecy is directed to the Roman Catholic Church and its leaders.

Here is another prophecy that was given by Saint John Bosco: "Suddenly the pope falls gravely wounded. Immediately, those who are with him run to help him and they lift him up. ... A shout of victory and joy rings out amongst the enemies; from their ships an unspeakable mockery arises."[5] [Some believe this message prophesies the attempted assassination of Pope John Paul II.]

OUR LADY OF FATIMA

On May 13, 1917, in a field near Fatima, Portugal, three children reported that they were witnesses of an apparition of the Virgin Mary. The children were Lucia Dos Santos (aged ten), and her two cousins, Francisco (aged nine) and Jacinta Marti (aged seven).

The children said that Mary told them when she would appear again. On five subsequent occasions crowds of people flocked to Fatima in order to experience what they believed would be the miraculous manifestation of Mary. A crowd of nearly fifty thousand people gathered on October 13, 1917. Many of those present said that they witnessed a bright cloud over a beech tree, but only the three children could hear and see the "visitor from Heaven."

On that day the prophecy that has come to be known as "the Secret of Our Lady of the Rosary" was issued. Though it was a rainy day, journalists who were present said that the rain stopped suddenly and then the sun reappeared. One professor who was present said that the sun looked like "... a burnished wheel cut out of mother of pearl. This disc spun dizzily around.... It whirled upon itself with mad rapidity, then advanced, blood red, towards the Earth, threatening to crush us with its weight."[6]

Terrified spectators fell to their knees in prayer. Amazingly, the rain-soaked clothing of those present dried immediately when the sun came out.

THE LAST-POPE PROPHECY AND OTHER ROMAN CATHOLIC
PROPHECIES

The Secret of Our Lady of the Rosary consists of three parts. According to the children, Mary ordered them to keep the prophecy secret for at least twenty-five years, or until after the death of Lucia.

Francisco and Jacinta died during the influenza epidemic of 1918-1919. Lucia went on to become a cloistered Carmelite nun. After learning to write, she recorded the words of the prophecy, which was kept in the Bishopric of Leiria until 1943. In that year Pope Pius XII revealed the first two parts of the prophecy.

The first section presents a vision of hell. The second part is purported to have predicted World War II. The third section was opened by Pope John XXIII and several cardinals in 1960. According to some reports, the pope actually fainted when he read the final section of the prophecy.

The pope and some cardinals eventually "leaked" the third "secret" to certain Roman Catholic officials and some world leaders. Here are some excerpts that were published by the German journal *News Europe* on October 15, 1963. (Though the text cannot be absolutely verified, it is believed to be genuine.)

"The time of times will come and everything will come to an end if humanity is not converted, and if things remain as they are now or get worse, the great and powerful men will perish just as will the small and weak.

"For the church, too, the time of its greatest trial will come. Cardinals will oppose cardinals and bishops against bishops. Satan will march in their midst and there will be great changes in Rome. What is rotten will fall, never to rise again. The church will be darkened and the world will shake with terror. The time will come when no king, emperor, cardinal or bishop will await Him who will, however, come, but in order to punish according to the designs of my Father.... [It is not hard to understand that a pope—the Bishop of Rome—might faint upon reading these words about the Roman Catholic Church.]

"A great war will break out.... Fire and smoke will fall from heaven, and waters of the oceans will become vapors, the scum will arise in a confused manner, and everything will sink down. Millions and millions of men will perish while this is going on and those who survive will envy the dead. The unexpected will follow in every part of the world, anxiety, pain and misery in every country. Have I seen it? The time is getting nearer and the abyss is getting wider without hope. The good will perish with the bad, the great with the small, the heads of the church with their faithful, and the rulers with their people....."[7]

This is a very dismal prophecy, indeed. So dismal, in fact, that Pope John Paul II said, "Due to the seriousness of the contents of the Fatima secret, my predecessors in the Throne of Peter have preferred to postpone the publication. Furthermore, it may be enough to the Christian people to know that, if there is a message saying that the oceans will flood whole parts of the globe, and millions of people will die from a minute to another, it is not really the case to will the publication of this secret message."[8]

The Roman Catholic Church finally published an official document entitled "The Message of Fatima" in June 2000. It includes the first and second part of "The Secret," and a photocopy of the original manuscript of the third part.

PADRE PIO

Well-known for the stigmata (bleeding wounds of Christ) in his hands, Padre Pio da Petrecina (1887-1968) transcribed several prophecies that he said were from Mary. (Concerning the stigmata, it is reported that he bled a cup of blood daily for fifty years.)

The following are excerpts from a letter that Padre Pio wrote to the Commission of Heroldsbach, which was appointed by the Vatican to investigate the miracles and visions of the priest. It is written as though the Lord was speaking directly to him:

"My son, my son, I have been longing for this hour in which I shall reveal to you the great love of my heart.... Pray and make reparation to me. Admonish others to do the same because the time is near at hand in which I shall visit my unfaithful people because they have not heeded the time of my grace. Persevere in prayer, so that your adversary [Satan] shall have no dominion over you. Tell my people to be prepared at all times, for my judgment shall come upon them suddenly and when least expected—and not one shall escape my hands. I shall find them all! I shall protect the just. Watch the sun and the moon and the stars of the heavens. When they appear to be unduly disturbed and restless, know that the day is not far away. Stay united in prayer and watching until the angel of destruction has passed your doors. Pray that these days will be shortened."[9] (This prophecy was received by Padre Pio in 1949.)

The other prophecies that were written down by Padre Pio are filled with calls to repentance. On February 7, 1950, he received this message: "Again and again I have warned men, and often have I given them special opportunities to return to the right path; but now, wickedness has reached its climax, and the punishment can no longer be delayed. Tell all that the time has come in which these things shall be fulfilled."[10]

SISTER AGNES SASAGAWA

The following prophecy has been approved by the Roman Catholic Church. It was reportedly received by a Japanese nun in 1969. Sister Agnes Sasagawa was a postulant in the Order of the Handmaids of the Eucharist. Sister Agnes, who was deaf, stated that she miraculously heard a voice urging her to go and pray in the chapel.

Sister Agnes received prophetic messages over a period of nine years. In 1973, she heard these words: "If men do not repent and better themselves, the Father will inflict a terrible punishment on all humanity. It will be a punishment greater than the deluge, such as one will never have seen before. Fire will fall from the sky and wipe out a great part of humanity, the good as well as the bad, sparing neither priests nor faithful. The survivors will find themselves so desolate that they will envy the dead.... In order that the world might know His anger, the heavenly Father is preparing to inflict a great chastisement on all mankind."[11]

The recurring theme of God's judgment falling upon mankind unless people repent is seen in many of the prophecies that have come from the Roman Catholic Church. We see this theme reiterated in the following prophecy, as well.

OUR MOTHER OF THE WORD

It is reported that Mary and Christ appeared to some Catholics in Kihebo, Rwanda, in November 1981. Here is one of the messages that was reportedly received by a visionary named Emmanuel: "There isn't much time left in preparing for the Last Judgment. We must change our lives; renounce sin. Pray and prepare for our own death and for the end of the world. We must prepare while there is still time. Those who do well will go to Heaven. If they do evil, they will condemn themselves with no hope of appeal. Do not lose time in doing good and praying. There is not much time and Jesus will come."[12]

Here we see the emphasis placed on preparing for the Last Judgment and getting ready for the Return of Jesus Christ.

At this same time, these Rwandans reported that they saw a vision that was related to their nation. The vision lasted eight hours, and in it they saw horrible images of tragedy, including massacres, decapitated bodies, and bodies being thrown into rivers. This vision was fulfilled a few years later when the Rwandan holocaust took place.

VERONICA LUEKEN

According to Veronica Lueken of Flushing Meadows Park, New York, both Jesus and Mary appeared to her repeatedly over a period of twenty-five years. She said that she received a harsh warning from the Virgin Mary; it proclaimed that unless people return to traditional morals, World War III and a great comet will kill billions of people.

During a moment of religious ecstasy, on April 21, 1973, Veronica said she received another warning. This is how she described it: "It's as though everything has exploded in the sky. There is a great flash! Then it's very hot—very warm—and it feels like you're burning. There is a huge explosion, and the sky becomes very white ... and then there are colors.... Now this voice—the voice!... Our Lady says, '... warning before the chastisement. Flash, fire, and the voice within you! The final warning before chastisement.... Many signs of an angry God will appear before you."[13]

Each of these Roman Catholic prophecies seems to have an "escape clause" that is based on people repenting of their sins. To repent means to feel sorry for one's sins to the extent that the sinner determines to change his or her behavior completely, and to start walking in the direction of righteousness.

THE LAST-POPE PROPHECY

Saint Malachy was born in AD 1094 in Armagh, Ireland. He was canonized as the first Irish saint by Pope Clement III in AD 1190. He predicted his own death, which occurred on November 2, 1148, at which time he died in the arms of his good friend Saint Bernard of Clairvaux.

There is a direct correlation between the prophecies of Saint Malachy and the Mayan Long-count Calendar, which ends on December 21, 2012. Let's now see what this prophet had to say about future popes.

While on a visit to Rome in AD 1139, Malachy said he received a vision of all the popes who would ever reign (112 popes in all). After seeing these popes in the vision, he wrote down a series of Latin phrases that described each pope. These phrases were like mottos that had something to do with each pope's name or ministry. He listed each one according to various epigrams, such as "the tears of the sun."

Reportedly, Malachy gave his report to Pope Innocent II in 1140. Then, according to researchers, it was "lost" in the Vatican for four hundred years, only to be rediscovered in AD 1595.

It is said that the Vatican holds very closely to Saint Malachy's prophecy.

THE FINAL TEN POPES

Here is the list of the final ten popes and the epigrams Malachy used to identify each one. Of course, he did not know the actual names of the popes, but discussed them in terms of these epigrams.

1. *The Burning Fire* (*Ignis Ardens*—Pope Pius X (1903-1914). The burning passion (ardent fire) of this particular pope was to bring spiritual renewal to the church—the fires of revival, if you will. He was known for his personal piety and his zeal in fighting modernism in the church. He became the first pope in more than four centuries to be canonized as a saint.

2. *Religion Laid Waste* (*Religio Depopulata*)—Benedict XV (1914-1922). It was during Benedict's reign that communism moved into Russia, where religion was truly laid waste under the atheistic regime. During this pope's rule, also, World War

I took place, and millions of Christians were killed. The great
influenza pandemic, which killed millions of people, took
place during his rule, as well. He truly presided over an era
when it seemed that everything was laid waste.

3. *Unshaken Faith (Fides Intrepida)*—Pope Benedict XV
(1922-1939). Unshaken faith seems to be an accurate description
of this pope, who faced tremendous pressure from Fascist and
other political powers in Germany and Italy. He was a very
vocal critic of both Communism and Fascism, and he even
aroused the ire of Adolf Hitler. He released the encyclical *Mit
Brennender Sorge*, which condemned Nazi racism.

4. *An Angelic Shepherd (Pastor Angelicus)*—Pope Pius XII
(1939-1958). This very mystical prelate was deeply spiritual
and seemed to have a "pastor's heart." It is reported that he
had received visions that have not been made public. Peter
Bander writes this description of him, "... he has emerged as
one of the great popes of all time.... [he] was in the truest sense
of the word an angelic pastor to the flock...."

5. *Pastor and Mariner (Pastor et Nauta)*—John XXIII
(1958-1963). Like his predecessor, John was a true pastor
and shepherd; prior to his appointment as pope, he was the
Patriarch of Venice—a city on the sea, hence the reference
to a mariner. It is said that Cardinal Spellman (of New York
City), during the conclave which was to elect the next pope,
in response to Saint Malachy's prophecy about him, rented a
boat, filled it with sheep, and sailed up and down the Tiber
River.

6. *Flower of Flowers (Flos Florum)*—Paul VI (1963-
1978). Paul's coat-of-arms depicts three *fleurs-de-lis*—iris
blossoms. The *fleur-de-lis* is symbolic of purity and chastity
in the Catholic religion. This pope condemned artificial birth
control.

7. *Of the Half Moon (De Medietate Lunae)*—John Paul I
(1978-1978). This pope was elected on August 26, 1978, when
there was a half moon. He was also born on the day of the

POPE BENEDICT XVI

half-moon (October 17, 1912). He reigned for only thirty-three days, approximately one month. (Some believe he may have been murdered, but this is pure conjecture.)

8. *The Labor of the Sun* (*De Labore Solis*)—John Paul II (1978-2005). Pope John Paul II, noted for his frequent world travels, his deep spirituality, and his kindness, was the only pope who was born on the day of a solar eclipse. During World War II he worked in a quarry in his native Poland, laboring every day in the sunlight. He was entombed when the sun was eclipsed, as well. He was the first non-Italian elected to the

papacy in more than four centuries. Like the sun, which never ceases its important work, Pope John Paul II was incessant in his work. He compared abortion to the Holocaust and denounced gay marriage. An assassination attempt on his life failed, and he even went to the prison where the man who shot him was incarcerated, and the pope forgave him.

9. *The Glory of the Olive (De Gloria Olivae)*—Benedict XVI (2005-present). The first Saint Benedict prophesied that before the end of the world his order (the Benedictines, which are also known as the Olivetans) will triumphantly lead the church. The olive branch is both a symbol of peace and an emblem for the Jews. It is also a symbol for the Benedictines. It is believed by some that this pope will reign during a peaceful era when many Jews will be converted to faith in Jesus Christ. It is interesting to note that Jesus gave one of His homilies on the end times from the Mount of Olives.

[Pope Benedict XVI is the 265th Pope of the Roman Catholic Church. He is now an octogenarian and may not rule much longer.]

10. *Peter the Roman.* The last pope is actually given a name by Saint Malachy (or someone else), who wrote, "In the final persecution of the Holy Roman Church there will reign Petrus Romanus, who will feed his flock amid many tribulations; after which the seven-hilled city [Rome] will be destroyed and the dreadful Judge will judge the people. The End."[14]

There are those who say that Peter the Roman was added to the list of popes many years after Malachy recorded his original prophecy. As a consequence, many think that Pope Benedict XVI may well be the last pope.

In 1909, Pope Pius X said he had a vision from which he quickly "awoke" and cried, "What I see is terrifying. Will it be myself? Will it be my successor? What is certain is that the pope will quit Rome, and in leaving the Vatican, he will have to walk over the dead bodies of his priests."[15]

A PROPHECY OF SAINT HILDEGARD

Saint Hildegard (Twelfth Century)—"Before the comet comes, many nations, the good excepted, will be scourged by want and famine. The great nation in the ocean that is inhabited by people of different tribes and descent will be devastated by earthquake, storm, and tidal wave. It will be divided, and, in great part, submerged. That nation will also have many misfortunes at sea and lose its colonies.

"After the great comet, the great nation will be devastated by earthquakes, storms, and great waves of water, causing much want and plagues. The ocean will also flood many other countries, so that all coastal cities will live in fear, with many destroyed.

"All seacoast cities will be fearful, and many of them will be destroyed by tidal waves, and most living creatures will be killed, and even those who escape will die from a horrible disease. For in none of those cities does a person live according to the Laws of God.

"A powerful wind will rise in the North, carrying heavy fog and the densest dust, and it will fill their throats and eyes so that they will cease their butchery and be stricken with a great fear."[16]

A scientific report was released by nearly two thousand climate researchers and leading scientists meeting in Copenhagen in March, 2009, who warned that global warming "…is accelerating beyond the worst predictions and threatening to trigger 'irreversible' climate shifts on the planet." These researchers seem to confirm what Saint Hildegard predicted during the twelfth century.

They have urged leaders of world governments to "vigorously" implement strategies to cut emissions of heat-trapping greenhouse gases. They predict a rise in the sea level of possibly twenty-three to thirty-nine inches by the end of the twenty-first century, which would bring massive flooding to many low-lying regions of the Earth.[17]

"Since the whole world is against God and His church, it is evident that He has reserved the victory over His enemies to himself. This will be more obvious when it is considered that the root of all our present evils is to be found in the fact that those with talents and vigor crave earthly pleasures, and not only desert God but repudiate Him altogether. Thus it appears they cannot be brought back in any other way except through an act that cannot be ascribed to any secondary agency, and thus all will be forced to look to the supernatural....

"There will come a great wonder, which will fill the world with astonishment. This wonder will be preceded by the triumph of revolution. The church will suffer exceedingly. Her servants and her chieftain will be mocked, scourged, and martyred" (Pope Pius IX in 1878).[18]

ENDNOTES

1. *Why Last Pope.* http://www.whylastpope.com/end.htm
2. *Marian Apparitions and Prophecies.* http://www.rexresearch. com/mary/maryapps.htm
3. Ibid.
4. Ibid.
5. Ibid.
6. Ibid.
7. Ibid.
8. Ibid.
9. Ibid.
10. Ibid.
11. Ibid.
12. Ibid.

13. Ibid.

14. *Malachy's Prophecies—the Last 10 Popes.* http://bibleprobe.com/last10popes.htm

15. Ibid.

16. Ibid.

17. http://news.aol.com/article/climate-changes/376821

18. *Malachy's Prophecies—the Last 10 Popes.* http://bibleprobe.com/last19popes.htm

Other Resources That Were Consulted in the Preparation of This Chapter

1. *Prophecy of St. Malachy—Is Ratzinger the Doomsday Pope?* http://www.satansrapture.com/pope112.htm

2. *Saint Malachy.* http://en.wikipedia.org/wiki/Saint_Malachy

3. *Prophecy of the Popes.* http://en.wikipedia.org/wiki/Prophecy_of_the_Popes

4. *The Last Pope Revisited.* http:www.hogueprophecy.com/bookpromo/lastpopedesc.htm

Additional Resources You May Wish to Explore

1. *The Meaning of Fatima* by C.C. Martindale. Published by P.J. Kennedy & Sons, New York, 1950.

2. *Encountering Mary: Visions From La Salette to Medjugorje* by Sandra Zimdars-Swartz. Published by Queenship Publishing, Santa Barbara, California.

THE POLE-SHIFT THEORY AND OTHER SCIENTIFIC PREDICTIONS

We know, for example, that every once in awhile something truly mind-boggling, almost unthinkable, happens.
For reasons that are still not fully understood, our familiar north and south poles trade places—the magnetic field of the Earth does a complete flip-flop. Although polar reversals are rare in the history of civilizations, the geologic record shows that they happen routinely in terms of Earth's history. Magnetic reversals have already happened 171 times in the last 76 million years, with at least 14 of those reversals occurring in the last 4.5 million years alone.
FROM "CHOICE POINT 2012—OUR DATE WITH THE WINDOW OF EMERGENCE," BY GREGG BRADEN[1]

POLAR REORIENTATION

The Pole-shift Theory is a scientific hypothesis that is based on geological research. It states that the axis of rotation of the Earth (which goes through the North and South Poles) has not always been in its present location. This implies that the location of the axis may change in the future, as well. According to many scientists, the physical poles of our planet could well be getting ready for another shift.

IT IS POSSIBLE THAT CENTRIFUGAL FORCE FROM THE EARTH'S
ROTATION COULD BRING THE ICE CAPS DOWN TO THE
EQUATOR AT SOME POINT IN THE FUTURE.

An early proponent of this theory was Hugh Auchincloss
Brown, an electrical engineer who put forth a proposition
regarding the potential for a catastrophic pole shift. Brown's
theory is based on monitoring the accumulation of ice at both
poles. He said that this accumulation of ice causes a recurring
tipping of the axis in cycles that are approximately seven
millennia long. The tipping he refers to, therefore, stems from
the weight of ice accumulating at both poles.

Another proponent of this theory was Charles Hapgood, who wrote *The Earth's Shifting Crust* (1958), which includes a foreword by Albert Einstein, and *Path of the Pole* (1970). Hapgood took Brown's theory a bit farther by speculating that the ice mass at one or both poles can over-accumulate and destabilize the Earth's rotational balance. When and if this happens, all or much of Earth's outer crust around the planet's core could slip and cause a reorientation of the poles.

Hapgood's research led him to believe that these shifts take approximately five thousand years to develop, and they are followed by twenty to thirty thousand years of no polar movements. He concluded that the North Pole has been located in several different places throughout the history of the Earth; some of those places were the Yukon Territory, the Hudson Bay, and the Atlantic Ocean between Iceland and Norway.[2]

It is said that Albert Einstein was "electrified" by Hapgood's theories. Einstein and Hapgood accepted the idea that the Earth's crust "floats" on a turbulent, molten lava ocean. The turbulence is caused by the fact that the Earth's core is spinning faster than the crust of the Earth is, and the molten lava beneath the Earth's crust is a force that causes many natural disasters.

In fact, the source for every volcano, earthquake, tsunami, and polar shift is found beneath the Earth's crust, and these forces are often related to lunar phases. Many believe that earth shifts are most likely to occur around the time of very high tides, and cataclysmic natural events could be governed by the "tides" within the lava ocean beneath the Earth's crust.

It is believed by some that ice build-up at the polar caps could cause the Earth's crust to slide over the underlying lava ocean. It is possible, therefore, that centrifugal force from the Earth's rotation could bring the ice caps down to the equator at some point in the future. There is some geological evidence to suggest that this has happened before. Indeed, it may have happened over one-hundred-and-seventy times during the "life" of the Earth.

Let's delve into this a bit further: A critical mass of ice, joining with a strong influence from the moon, could trigger the next polar shift. If this happens, we can expect devastating earthquakes, volcanoes, and tsunamis that will go beyond anything we can possibly envision.

Imagine, if you will, a tsunami so powerful that it would cover the Himalayan Mountains in moments. This would be a flood that would seemingly exceed biblical proportions—a flood so devastating that life on our planet would be completely destroyed.

GLOBAL WARMING

What is being called "global warming" is apparently not causing a reduction in the ice masses at the poles, even though ice shelves are breaking away rapidly. The chunks of ice floating in the oceans do nothing to create a polar imbalance. Instead, a rise of temperature in the polar regions increases the amount of snowfall in those areas, because warmer air carries and deposits more moisture than cold air. Therefore, even though ice shelves are melting and breaking away, snow, water, and ice masses are simultaneously causing a rapid re-accumulation of ice in the polar regions.

These changes are gradual, but they are not imperceptible. In truth, they are measurable, and recent measurements help us to understand the reality of this phenomenon.

There are certain experts who believe that these changes will happen very rapidly, and these scientists believe that such transitions will result in dramatic upheavals in geography due to major earthquakes and tsunamis. Some even go so far as to suggest that these upheavals could take place in weeks, days, or even hours. Whatever the case, it is clear that any polar shifts will cause dramatic changes in climate all over the Earth.

Equatorial areas will become temperate, and temperate areas will become more equatorial or more frigid.

WILL A POLAR REVERSAL OR POLAR SHIFT OCCUR IN 2012?

While a polar shift may move the poles only forty degrees or less, a polar reversal would actually move the location of the North Pole to the location of the South Pole and vice-versa.

Patrick Geryl writes, "In 2012 the next polar reversal will take place on earth. This means that the North Pole will be changed into the South Pole. Scientifically this can only be explained by the fact that the earth will start rotating in the opposite direction, together with a huge disaster of unknown proportions."[3]

Unlike many scientists, Geryl believes that the rotation of the Earth is not stable. He bases his theory about this upon his research into ancient hieroglyphs, codes, maps, and other sources. Here are his conclusions:

1. Sudden polar reversals and shifts are natural. However, they could well result in massive destruction.

2. Polar reversals come about as a result of the harmonic cycles of the sun's magnetic fields.

3. Polar reversals can be predicted with some degree of accuracy on the basis of sunspot theories and magnetic field theories, which the Mayans and ancient Egyptians seemed to have understood.

Here is Geryl's description of what will happen on Earth as a result of a polar reversal:

"… life after a polar reversal is nothing but horror, pure unimaginable horror. All securities you presently have at hand, like—amongst others—food, transport, and medicines, will have disappeared in one big blow, dissolved into nothingness."[4]

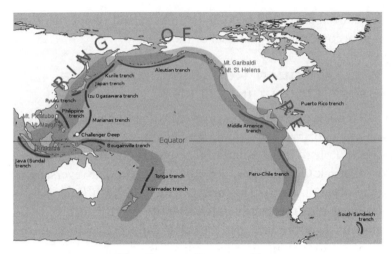

THE PACIFIC RING OF FIRE

A VOLCANIC ERUPTION ON KILAUEA, HAWAII

THE RING OF FIRE

The mountainous "ring of fire" (volcanic mountains—
some active—that nearly encircle the Pacific Ocean) is believed
to be aligned with the lunar tides. These mountains "float" on
a sea of molten lava in the same way that icebergs float in the
oceans. If an iceberg sinks into the ocean, it displaces the water
of the sea that surrounds it. Similarly, if a mountain in the Ring
of Fire sinks into the sea of molten lava, it will displace the
lava that is beneath it. It is easy to see how this would produce
earthquakes and fault-line movements, especially since the
Ring of Fire coincides with the edges of one of the world's
main tectonic plates. More than half of the world's volcanoes
are found within the Ring of Fire.

It is believed that the Ring of Fire is affected by the lunar
and solar tides; sometimes this happens when the moon is at
its closest point to the Earth. If this takes place when trillions
of tons of ice and snow have built up on the land masses near
the poles, it is likely that a polar shift would occur in response
to land movements resulting from volcanic activity.

There are those who believe we are close to such an
occurrence. In fact, some, including Patrick Geryl, are saying
that they believe a polar shift will occur sometime during the
year 2012. Whenever it takes place, however, it is clear that
many parts of the Earth will experience a new Ice Age. It will
be a time of intense cold, and this could well bring an end to
life on Earth.

Gregg Braden, a writer and researcher, who wrote several
best-selling books and studied remote cultures and their secrets
for many years, writes as follows about magnetic reversals of
the poles: "And while they are definitely cyclic, the reversals
appear to vary in time, making the time of the next one an
uncertainty. There are symptoms, however, that precede the
flip-flops, such as abrupt changes in weather patterns and
a rapid weakening of the planets' magnetic field—both of

THE BEE POPULATION HAS DECLINED DRAMATICALLY IN THE
UNITED STATES AND ELSEWHERE.

which are happening right now. It is the appearance of these symptoms today, and the fact that we are 'overdue' for a polar shift, that has led a growing number of mainstream scientists to suggest that we are in the early stages of such a reversal."[5]

Will it happen in 2012?

VANISHING BEE COLONIES

Albert Einstein said, "If the bee disappeared off the surface of the globe then man would only have four years of life left. No more bees, no more pollination, no more plants, no more animals, no more man." Has the disappearance of the bee already begun?[6]

Without any doubt, we are witnessing a dramatic decline in the bee population of the United States and elsewhere, and this will definitely have an impact on the production of crops in the Western Hemisphere. Bees in the United States pollinate more than fourteen billion dollars worth of crops and seeds annually.

Some European nations are experiencing similar declines of their bee populations. Investigators call this phenomenon "Colony Collapse Disorder" (CCD).[7]

Why are we losing our bees? In all likelihood, multiple causations are at work here. One contributing factor may be that modern agricultural practices have weakened the immune systems of bees. It is quite possible that genetically modified crops have played a role, as well. Other factors may include stress and parasites.

Dennis van Englesdorp from the Pennsylvania Department of Agriculture compares what is happening to the bees to the AIDS epidemic in humans. This analogy helps us to understand how serious the problem with the bees has become in that AIDS is a terminal illness, as is the problem that is impacting the bees.[8]

Some believe that quantum-mechanical effects related to magnetic fields and electromagnetic waves help to explain the loss of bees in the United States. The effects of these fields and waves may make it impossible for the bees to find their way back to their hives. Some suspect that mobile phones may even play a role in this; others believe it stems from solar activity, such as sunspots.

German researchers have determined that bees show a definite change of behavior when they are near power lines, and a study that was conducted at Landau University revealed that bees avoided returning to their hives when mobile phones were placed near them. As a result, the bees died without being able to return home.[9]

The mathematician Barbara Shipman suggests that the hub of most bee activity is related to finding pollen and returning to the hive. Upon finding a food source and returning to the hive, bees perform a dance that explains to other members of the colony where the food may be found. According to Shipman, the dance is influenced by various factors, such as sunlight and variations in the Earth's magnetic field.[10]

At least one thing that Shipman says is fairly certain: bees appear to be very sensitive to any fluctuations of energy in their environments. One study, for example, reveals that bees are highly sensitive to nuclear magnetic resonance. Such resonance occurs when an electromagnetic wave alters the orientation of the nuclei of atoms.

Some scientists are convinced that the next solar maximum (caused by sunspots that generate great magnetism) may be the most intense one that has ever occurred. At least one astronomer, Mausumi Dikpati, who works at the National Center for Atmospheric Research, predicts that the next solar maximum will occur in 2012. Dikpati believes that this phenomenon could affect electronics, such as GPS systems and mobile phones.[11] Solar Cycle 24 began in 2007, and this may help to account for the decline in the bee population, as well.

At least one thing is certain: the next solar cycle will be huge. Solar physicist David Hathaway of the Marshall Space Flight Center writes that Solar Cycle 24, which is due to peak in 2010 or 2011, "… looks like it's going to be one of the most intense cycles since record-keeping began almost 400 years ago." He and his colleague, Robert Wilson, base their forecast on historical records of geomagnetic storms.[12]

Hathaway writes, "When a gust of solar wind hits Earth's magnetic field, the impact causes the magnetic field to shake. If it shakes hard enough, we call it a geomagnetic storm." Such storms could cause power outages and make compass needles swing in the wrong directions. They also generate beautiful displays of the Aurora Borealis and other auroras.

The Science Editor for London's *Daily Mail*, Michael Hanlon, wrote an article entitled "Meltdown," which was published on April 20, 2009. Hanlon writes, "The catastrophe, when it comes, will be beautiful at first. It is a balmy evening in late 2012. Ever since the sun set, the dimming skies over London have been alive with fire.

"Pillars of incandescent green writhe like gigantic serpents across the skies. Sheets of orange race across the horizon during the most spectacular display of the Aurora Borealis seen in southern England for 153 years.

"And then, 90 seconds later, the lights start to go out. Not the lights in the sky—they will dazzle until dawn—but the lights on the ground."

The editor goes on to describe in great detail the disastrous scenario that will take place after the predicted solar superstorm of 2012:

- No electricity
- No food
- No TV
- No radio
- No telephones
- No internet
- No medicines
- No manufacturing
- No farming

He further predicts that 100,000 Europeans will die of starvation by the end of 2013. Hanlon says that it will take two decades or more for plant life to return.

Hanlon concludes his article by saying, "Perhaps it would be wise to start stocking up on some candles."

GALACTIC ALIGNMENT

What is a galactic alignment? This term refers to an alignment between the December solstice sun with the Milky Way, which is known as the "equator of our galaxy." This is an event that will coincide with the end of the Mayan calendar— December 21, 2012.

The alignment will take place because of the precession of the equinoxes. (See Chapter 1.) This precession is caused by the Earth wobbling on its axis very slowly, resulting in the

LUCAS JENNINGS' 1625 ENGRAVING OF OUROBOROS,
AND A SYMBOLIC FORM OF OUROBOROS.

shifting of the position of the equinoxes and solstices by one degree every 71.5 years.

There is considerable debate regarding when this galactic alignment will take place. Some believe it already has occurred. However, John Major Jenkins writes, "Amazingly, the center of this cosmic cross, that is, right where the elliptic crosses over the Milky Way, *is exactly where the December solstice sun will be in AD 2012.* This alignment occurs only once every 25,800 years. [The Mayan calendar pointed this out, as well.]

"The bottom line of my theory is that the ancient Maya chose the 2012 end-date because this is the date on which occurs a rare alignment of the solstice sun with the Galactic Center.

"The Long-count calendar is a galactic calendar because it pinpoints a rare alignment with our Milky Way Galaxy, due to occur in AD 2012—a date written as 13.0.0.0.0 in the long count."[13]

Jenkins actually puts forth several different dates for this cosmic event to occur, but seems to stress the likelihood of it taking place in 2012.

Ouroboros

The myth of *Ouroboros* (a Greek term that means "devouring its own tail") apparently originated in Egypt around 1600 BC. It refers to a serpent of light that resides in the heavens. The Milky Way represents this serpent, and it is viewed at a galactic central point near Sagittarius. This view shows the serpent eating its own tail. (Comparable myths are also found in Norse and Hindu mythology.)

The Egyptian myth prophesies that the Milky Way time cycle will end in catastrophic change. It further suggests that the sun will rise out of the mouth of Ouroboros, and this will take place on the winter solstice—December 21, 2012.

The Greeks gave a name to this end of the age; they called it the *Suntelia Aion*. Many ancient philosophers and historians, including Plato, discussed this cycle of catastrophe that would take place at the end of the age.

This myth has several meanings, but most of all it suggests the cyclic nature of the universe—destruction followed by creation and death followed by new life, etc. It can also symbolize eternity—the never-ending circle of life.

Sir Thomas Browne, a physician who was also an alchemist, wrote, "... that the first day should make the last, that the tail of the snake should return into its mouth precisely at the same time, and that they should wind up upon the day of their nativity, is indeed a remarkable coincidence."

In *The Garden of Cyrus* (1658) Browne wrote, "All things began in order so shall they end, so shall they begin again according to the Ordainer of Order and the mystical mathematics of the City of Heaven."[14]

On Aztec and Toltec ruins, the god Quetzalcoatl is sometimes portrayed as an Ouroboros.

Has Ouroboros begun to eat its tail?

HUMAN BEHAVIOR AND THE ELLIOTT WAVE PRINCIPLE

The Elliott Wave Principle was formulated by Ralph Nelson Elliott during the 1930's and 1940's. This principle describes how groups of people behave. It suggests that mass psychology is often at work behind the scenes, and this psychology (or a collective subconscious) is responsible for certain human behaviors.

Such changes in behavior appear to come in waves or eras. For example, a wave of pessimism may be followed by a wave of optimism. Frequently, these waves swing back and forth like a pendulum.

The movements of these waves can often be traced to the world's financial markets. According to Elliott, the behavior of investors is influenced by the Wave Principle, and this can be tracked by the rise and fall of prices in the stock markets. Sometimes investors make their investment decisions according to the movement of these waves and patterns.[15]

When people are optimistic about the future, they will bid stock prices up. Markets do not react consistently to news related to outside events, however. Sometimes external news will drive the markets up, while at other times it will drive the markets down. Markets appear to move in waves, and there is evidence to suggest that these waves follow the Elliott Wave Principle.

Some theorists believe that the year 2012 will be preceded by a major financial collapse. As we know, there is a global recession in the world today. Is it possible that this recession will become a depression in 2012? An economist at Harvard University, Jeffrey Frankel, believes the economy follows a biblical pattern: "Seven fat years followed by seven lean years." He says that capital flows into developing economies according to a fifteen-year pattern.[16]

The year between the two seven-year phases is when the flow of money stops. Are we in the seven-lean-year phase? Will the flow of money stop in 2012? Frankel says there have been two such cycles in the recent past. According to him, the next major blow to emerging-market economies will come in 2011 or 2012.

THE DOOMSDAY CLOCK

The Doomsday Clock has been maintained by the Board of Directors of the *Bulletin of the Atomic Scientists* at the University of Chicago in Chicago, Illinois, since 1947. At present, the Doomsday Clock says that we are five minutes

THE DOOMSDAY CLOCK ADVANCED BY TWO MINUTES ON
JANUARY 17, 2007, AND IT REMAINS POSITIONED AT FIVE
MINUTES TO MIDNIGHT.

to midnight. (Midnight is a figure of speech that represents catastrophic destruction.)

The massive destruction that the Doomsday Clock attempts to monitor used to refer only to nuclear devastation. Now, however, the measurement refers to other possible causes for a widespread catastrophe, such as environmental, biological, and technological threats to mankind.

The clock advanced by two minutes on January 17, 2007, and it remains positioned at five minutes to midnight. This change reflects various international events that the scientists involved perceive to be threats to mankind. These threats include North Korea's nuclear-weapon tests, Iran's quest for nuclear development, a renewed emphasis on nuclear weaponry by the U.S. military, the lack of security surrounding nuclear materials, and the existence of over twenty-six thousand nuclear weapons in the United States and Russia, not to mention others in Israel, India, Pakistan, China, Great Britain, France, etc.

Recent changes in climate have also been included in predictions related to the Doomsday Clock. The clock keeps ticking, and the changes in our environment are occurring at a rapid pace. According to these scientists, it's almost midnight, and when the clock strikes twelve, life on Earth will be over.

Sir Martin Rees, the English Astronomer Royal, recently said, "Humankind's collective impacts on the biosphere, climate and oceans are unprecedented. These environmentally driven threats—'threats without enemies'—should loom as large in the political perspective as did the East/West political divide during the Cold War era."

Perhaps we can set the clock back a bit by instituting better arms control, increasing international security, stimulating green-energies, reforming our governmental energy departments, expanding bio-defense research, combating diseases in the oceans, being vigilant with regard to terrorism, monitoring the spread of epidemics, and using energy sources wisely. At least we should try to do so.

The nuclear age began in the 1940's. This is when scientists learned how to release the energy that is stored within atoms. As with many things in nature, this new discovery brought forth a duality in the form of potential uses. Nuclear energy could be used to produce an unparalleled weapon and it could be used to provide relatively clean energy.

Though the Cold War is apparently over, nuclear knowledge and nuclear materials continue to circulate around the globe. When terrorists obtain such knowledge and materials, who knows what they will do? It seems highly likely that they would use them in the most destructive ways imaginable.

U.S. President Barack Obama recognizes the seriousness of this threat. He said, "A world without nuclear weapons is profoundly in America's interest and the world's interest. It is our responsibility to make the commitment, and to do the hard work to make this vision a reality."[17]

President of Iran,
Mahmoud
Ahmadinejad.

Nuclear energy could be used to produce an
unparalleled weapon.

How this might be accomplished is another matter altogether. China possesses four hundred nuclear warheads, France has three hundred forty-eight, and Israel and Britain have about two hundred each. The United States and Russia are the world's largest nuclear nations. These two countries together possess approximately 93 percent of the world's atomic weapons.

The International Panel on Fissile Materials tells us that highly enriched uranium, which is necessary for the production of a nuclear bomb, is found in more than forty nations that do not now have nuclear weapons. On every continent, with the exception of Antarctica, there is at least one nation that possesses highly enriched uranium. Concerns about the proliferation of this knowledge and these materials continue to grow.

Much of the world's attention is focused on Iran, because we know that this is a nation that is seeking to compete in the nuclear arena. Though Iranian leaders say they want to develop nuclear technology solely for non-military purposes, most world leaders are not convinced about this. The fact that the President of the Islamic Republic of Iran, Mahmoud Ahmadinejad, has stated that his nation will "wipe Israel off the map" makes everyone feel uneasy about their intentions.

It has also been estimated that approximately thirty countries possess the capabilities to develop an atomic bomb, though some of these may not have any intention of doing so.

CLIMATOLOGY

The Doomsday Clock also deals with matters related to the climate. Starting in the 1950's scientists began to measure the changes in the concentration of carbon dioxide in the atmosphere. According to scientists, that concentration of carbon dioxide is higher now than it has been in the past 650,000 years.[18]

What does this fact mean for the environment of the Earth? The gases in the atmosphere work like a giant blanket that keeps the warmth of the sun's heat within the atmosphere. This melts ice, and it triggers many ecological changes all over the planet. Some argue that the increase in carbon dioxide in the atmosphere is due to the gas being discharged from the oceans and is not due to mankind's use of fossil fuels. Whatever the case, an increase in measurable global temperature is occurring due to carbon dioxide in the atmosphere.

Some scientists have warned us that even if we were to cease using equipment and machines that release carbon dioxide into the atmosphere, we would still have a major problem on our hands, because the extra gases that already exist within the atmosphere will not dissipate for centuries. As a result, the prediction is that sea levels will rise considerably within this century.

The Intergovernmental Panel on Climate Change (IPCC) predicts that global warming of two to ten degrees Fahrenheit over the next one hundred years is likely. This, they believe, will result in a dramatic rise in sea level, vast coastal erosion, and major flooding in coastal cities such as New York.[19]

What we saw in New Orleans in the aftermath of Hurricane Katrina in 2005, will seem small in comparison to the widespread flooding that could well occur in other cities in the relatively near future.

A Mega Tsunami

Scientists have issued a specific warning of a mega tsunami that threatens to cause enormous damage to major cities in the United States, Great Britain, northern Africa, and the coastline cities of Europe. One particular island in the Canary chain (Cumbre Vieja), which is located off the western coast of Africa, is the site of an unstable volcano. If this volcano erupts, a huge chunk of the island will likely fall into the

Atlantic Ocean, causing great turbulence that will result in a mega tsunami—the largest ocean wave in recorded history.

Dr. Simon Day from the Benfield Greig Hazards Research Centre of the University College of London says, "If the volcano collapsed in one block of almost twenty cubic kilometers of rock, weighing five hundred billion tons—twice the size of the Isle of Wight—it would fall into water almost four miles deep and create an undersea wave two thousand feet tall. Within five minutes of the landslide, a dome of water about a mile high would form and then collapse, before the mega tsunami fanned out in every direction, traveling at speeds of up to five hundred miles per hour. A three-hundred-thirty foot wave would strike the western Sahara in less than an hour."[20]

A dome of water about a mile high! An undersea wave that is two thousand feet tall! Such natural phenomena exceed the limits of our imagination, for we have never seen such mighty waves of water. Water can be very beneficial, but in this scenario, water would be horrendously damaging and destructive. Some say that a massive tsunami like the one depicted above would literally swamp the entire east coast of the United States at least twenty miles inland. Everyone who lives on the coast would be wiped out and buildings would be pulverized by the wall of water.

Dr. Day suggests that the United States would be devastated in the following way: "It [the mega tsunami] will surge across the Atlantic at five hundred miles per hour in less than seven hours, engulfing the whole U.S. east coast with a wave almost two hundred feet high, sweeping away everything it its path up to twenty miles inland. Boston would be hit first, followed by New York, then all the way down the coast to Miami, the Caribbean, and Brazil."[21]

With regard to the city of London, Dr. Day speculates that the city would be inundated by the mighty wave. He says, "The Thames estuary is already subject to major tidal surges, and the mega tsunami could raise water levels by as much as twenty feet, with the surge traveling up the river at some 200 miles per hour."[22] If this were the case, most of London would be uninhabitable for many months.

Dr. Day concludes his prediction with this alarming statement: "It's not a question of 'if' Cumbre Vieja collapses, it's simply a question of 'when.'"[23]

Recent evidence suggests that a very devastating tsunami may have crashed into the region that is now New York, Long Island, and New Jersey around 3000 BC The evidence for this is buried under deep sediment in that region.

In 1929, the Grand Banks tsunami took place along the coast of Newfoundland. I killed two dozen people and snapped many transatlantic cables.

Atlantic tsunamis have occurred before and these were apparently caused by earthquakes, such as the one that would cause the collapse of Cumbre Vieja.

NEW PATHOGENS

As Hitler attempted to do during World War II, some devious groups could well be trying to develop dangerous novel pathogens that could kill individuals or wipe out entire populations. In 2001, researchers in Australia reported that they had accidentally created a new, very virulent strain of the mousepox virus. This happened as a result of their attempts to engineer new ways to achieve more effective rodent control.[24]

All kinds of new pathogens are possible as a result of the burgeoning field of bioengineering research. It is not difficult for an individual or a group to obtain fragments of genetic material (even through the mail or via the Internet). One wonders what would happen if such material got into the hands of a malevolent individual or a terrorist.

The Human Genome Project has enabled scientists to identify more than eighteen hundred genes that are associated with particular diseases. The mapping of the human genome in 2001 helps us to understand human physiology and anatomy more fully. Are we on the verge of creating Frankenstein's monster? Now that the ability to clone animals is commonplace, will the cloning of human beings be just around the corner?

The possibilities created by such medical and scientific developments are seemingly limitless. In the same way that wind, water, and sunlight have both beneficial and destructive potentials, the development of new medical technologies can either benefit or destroy mankind.

COSMIC COLLISIONS

There is an ancient myth about a planet named Nibiru (or Niburu) that, according to Sumerian language texts, enters our solar system every thirty-six hundred years. This mythological planet's orbit would take it between Jupiter and Mars before it would return to outer space. The myth states that the next passage of this "planet" will cause earthquakes, tidal waves, famines, diseases, meteorites, and volcanic eruptions.

The Sumerian people said that they gathered their knowledge of Nibiru from the Anunnaki (people who inhabited the planet Nibiru and came to Earth). According to the Sumerians, the planet will return to Earth in 2012, and this event will bring radical changes to our planet.[25]

Though the story of Nibiru is a myth, there is some reason to be concerned about celestial bodies impacting Earth and other extraordinary celestial possibilities. Not long ago, for example, a meteorite passed within forty-six thousand miles of our planet, and it had not been foreseen by any astronomers.

There is evidence to suggest that our entire solar system is becoming increasingly turbulent due to the fact that we are moving into an interstellar energy cloud, according to Russian planetary geophysicists. The cloud is energizing and destabilizing the atmospheres of all the planets. Some scientists predict that this will bring about a catastrophe of unprecedented proportions sometime between 2010 and 2012.

As we have already mentioned, solar activity is increasing, and we expect to see it peak in 2012. Sun storms affect storms on the Earth. The major hurricanes of 2005 (Katrina, William, and Rita) were concurrent with the sun's stormiest weeks during that year.

IMPACT EVENTS

Physicists from the University of California at Berkeley have postulated that dinosaurs and the majority of other species on Earth were extinguished by the impact of a comet, a meteor, or an asteroid millions of years ago. The same thing could happen to our planet again. Are we overdue for such a collision, which astronomers call an "impact event"?

Small objects from space frequently hit the Earth, but large asteroids rarely do. The last-known impact of an object of 10 km or more (in diameter) is believed to have happened approximately sixty-five million years ago. (It is believed that this impact wiped out the dinosaurs and many other animals.)

In AD 1490, ten thousand people in Shanxi Province, China, were killed by "a hail of falling stones." It is believed that this shower of space rocks was triggered by the breakup of a large asteroid high in the atmosphere.[26]

In AD 1908, the barren plains of Siberia were devastated by an explosion that probably resulted from an airburst from an asteroid or comet well above the Earth's surface. As a result, more than eighty million trees in a region that covered over eight hundred and thirty square miles were destroyed. Fortunately, this took place in a relatively unpopulated region.

One scientist, Eugene Shoemaker of the U.S. Geological Survey, has suggested that an event equivalent to the destructive power of the atomic bomb that destroyed Hiroshima occurs approximately once a year! Why do such huge explosions go unnoticed? It is because most of the Earth's surface is covered with water, and many of these impacts take place in the ocean. Also, a number of these explosions occur at relatively high altitudes instead of actually hitting the Earth.

Craters on the moon and our own planet, several recorded near-misses with celestial objects, and life-extinguishing impact events that have happened in the past make us wonder if such a cosmic collision could happen again. Though the probability is low, the possibility is always there.

The Mayan leader Chilam Balam of Tizimin prophesied, "The surface of the Earth will be moved. How can the people be protected, thus disturbed in the midst of the Earth, in the sculptured land of Ichcansiho.... According to the omens above the Earth and the prophecies, the disturbances of our land shall eventually turn back."[27]

After reading this chapter and particularly the last section, we are led to wonder what would happen if any of the scenarios portrayed here were to actually take place. Several things could occur if an asteroid or other celestial body would enter Earth's atmosphere. Of course, the size, speed, and composition of the object would be the chief determinants.

The object could simply burn up as it enters the atmosphere, or, as has happened before, it could destroy most if not all life forms, or it could burn up millions of trees. It could create a massive, destructive tsunami if it were to crash into the sea, or leave a huge crater if it hits the land (causing earthquakes and other disturbances). It could result in a very long "nuclear-type winter," or it could even split the Earth in two. Such a cosmic event would definitely bring immense changes to our planet and to mankind.

In this chapter we have looked at various scientific facts, theories, and possibilities. Some of the things that are described here would be the result of natural forces; others would be caused by human beings. Though we may not be able to do much about the natural phenomena, there is much we can do to avoid catastrophes that might be caused by mankind. We can prepare for both types of scenarios by being vigilant and proactive with regard to the way we treat our planet and one another.

When faced with any challenge, there are at least three possible responses:

1. We can be inactive, which means we do nothing. This is a very dangerous approach, as we saw during the Nazi Holocaust and several other disastrous events that have taken place throughout human history.

2. We can be reactive, which is most likely an emotional response stemming from fear or anger. Such an approach is negative and counter-productive, because it avoids the use of human reason and spirituality altogether. Fear immobilizes us and anger blinds us. Neither response, therefore, is desirable.

3. We can be proactive. This means we take positive action to do whatever we can to meet the challenge. If this approach is taken in a unified way, the world and its citizens will greatly benefit. Actually, the challenges we face can be very productive, indeed, for they spur us to take action to find the necessary solutions.

There are essentially two emotions that dominate the human condition: love and fear. The Apostle John speaks to this reality when he writes, *"There is no fear in love; but perfect love casteth out fear; because fear hath torment. He that feareth is not made perfect in love"* (1 John 4:18, KJV).

We can choose which of these emotions we will give ourselves to—love, which eradicates all fear; or fear, which torments us. It really is a daily choice that we must make.

Love for our planet and one another is what we need today rather than fear, for love will always propel us in the right direction—to help, to find answers, to look for the best, to seek truth, to remain open to possibilities, and to hope. It is only through love that we shall be able to prevail in the face of challenging circumstances, whatever they may be.

The year 2012 is rapidly approaching. Therefore, let's prepare ourselves for it by looking at the possibilities and taking proactive measures to meet its potential challenges. Let us determine to stay in love, to remain positive, and to look for answers to the dilemmas we face. There is much we can do in this process.

Baltasar Gracian writes, "All that really belongs to us is time; even he who has nothing else has that." Let's use the time we have to make this world a better place.

Carl Sandburg has given us some wise advice regarding time. He said, "Time is the coin of your life. It is the only coin you have, and only you can determine how it will be spent. Be careful lest you let other people spend it for you."

Endnotes

1. Braden, Gregg. *The Mystery of 2012*, Sounds True, Inc., Boulder, Colorado, 2007.
2. *Pole Shift by 2012?* http://www.poleshift2012.com/site/1516717/page/723472
3. *Pole Shift and Pole Reversal in 2012.* http://www.survive2012.com/geryl1.php
4. Ibid.
5. Braden, Gregg. *The Mystery of 2012*, Sounds True, Inc., Boulder, Colorado, 2007.
6. *Vanishing Bee Colonies, Doomsday Scenario, and Sunspots.* www.buzzle.com/articles/vanishing-bee-colonies-doomsday-scenarios-sunspots.html
7. Ibid.
8. Ibid.
9. Ibid.
10. Ibid.

11. Joseph, Lawrence E, *Apocalypse 2012*. Broadway Books, New York, 2007.

12. *Solar Maximum.* http://2012wiki.com/index.php?title=Solar_Maximum

13. *Galactic Alignment,* http://2012wiki.com/index.php?title=Galactic_Alignment.

14. Browne, Thomas, *The Garden of Cyrus,* 1658.

15. *Elliott Wave.* http://2012wiki.com/index.php?title=Elliott_Wave

16. Ibid.

17. *Doomsday Clock May Finally Stop Clicking.* http://www.commondreams.org/headline/2009/02/24

18. *Doomsday Clock Overview.* http://www.thebulletin.org/content/doomsday-clock/overview

19. Ibid.

20. *A Wave of Destruction Will Destroy America's East Coast.* http://www.rense.com/general56/tsu.htm

21. Ibid.

22. Ibid.

23. Ibid.

24. *Doomsday Clock Overview.* http://www.thebulletin.org/content/doomsday-clock/overview

25. *Nibiru (Planet).* http://en.wikipedia.org/wiki/Nibiru_(planet)

26. *Impact Event.* http://en.wikipedia.org/wiki/Impact_event

27. Benedict, Gerald, *The Mayan Prophecies for 2012.* Watkins Publishing, London, 2008.

Other Resources That Were Consulted in the Preparation of This Chapter

1. http://www.universetoday.com/2008/06/19/2012-planet-x-is-not-nibiru/

2. *Pole Shift.* http://2012wiki.com/index.php?title=Pole_shift

3. *What Is the Ouroboros?* http://www.dragon.org/chris/ouroboros.html

4. *Ouroboros.* http://en.wikipedia.org/wiki/Ouroboros
5. *Climate Resets 'Doomsday Clock.'* http://news.bbc.co.uk/2/hi/
   science/nature/6270871.stm
6. http://www.worldatlas.com/aatlas/infopage/ringfire.htm
7. http://www.nineplanets.org/meteorites.html

Additional Resources You May Wish to Explore

1. *The HAB Theory* by Allan W. Eckert. Published by Little
   Brown & Company, 1976.
2. *Atlantis Found* by Clive Cussler. Published by G.P. Putnam's
   Sons, 1999.
3. *Earth's Catastrophic Past and Future: a Scientific Analysis of
   Information Channeled by Edgar Cayce* by William Hutton
   and Jonathan Eagle. Published by Universal Publishers, Boca
   Raton, Florida, 2004.
4. *When Life Nearly Died: the Greatest Mass Extinction of All
   Time* by Michael J. Benton. Published by Thames and Hudson,
   2003.

10

ASIAN PROPHECIES FROM THE HINDUS, BUDDHISTS, AND ZOROASTRIANS

Whenever there is decay of righteousness . . . and there is exaltation of unrighteousness, then I myself come forth ... for the destruction of evil-doers, for the sake of firmly establishing righteousness, I am born from age to age.
KRISHNA—FROM THE FOURTH DISCOURSE OF THE BHAGAVAD GITA[1]

THE FOUR STAGES OF HINDUISM

Hinduism is an ancient religion and social system that now includes elements of Buddhism and other religions and philosophies. It began in India, and most of its current adherents live in the Indian subcontinent.

The teachings of Hinduism involve reincarnation, yoga, and meditation. It is one of the oldest and most complex religions in the world. There are approximately nine million Hindus in the world today.

A social system of castes arose out of Hinduism. These castes are based on occupational classes, as follows:
- Brahmin caste—priests
- Kshatriya caste—soldiers, king-warriors
- Vaishya caste—merchants, farmers, laborers, craftspeople
- Harijahn caste—the "untouchables"

Unlike many religions, there is no known founder of Hinduism. Some of the key concepts of this religion include:

• Karma—a law of cause and effect through which every person creates his or her destiny through thoughts, words, and deeds.

• Reincarnation—cycles of rebirth that are determined by the individual's karma. The circle of birth, death, and rebirth is known as *samsara*.

• Holy Writings—the scriptures of Hinduism include the following: the Vedas (four "books of knowledge") and the *Upanishads* (presents the concept that behind all gods is the ultimate reality—Brahman).

• *Ramayana* and *Mahabharata*—two epics which tell of the mythical incarnations of Vishnu. (The *Bhagavad Gita* is a part of the *Mahabharata* and is the most popular of all Hindu texts. It tells Hindus how they can reach Nirvana—the state of perfect blessedness.)

• The Puranas—This collection of literature contains myths, folklore, and legends related to the Hindu gods.

According to Hinduism, there are three paths to liberation from the wheel of life.

These paths may be followed to obtain detachment from the self-life, including physical and personal existence, and freedom from all pain and suffering. These three pathways are:

• The Way of Works—This is achieved through the fulfillment of social and religious obligations.

• The Way of Devotion—This is the most popular way. It involves acts of worship to the gods.

• The Way of Knowledge—This way strives for a sense of higher consciousness until one is ultimately united with Brahman. The stepping-stones to this way include the reading of philosophical writings, the practice of yoga, and participation in deep meditation.

Hindu cosmology consists of four different stages. The universe is seen as being cyclical, as it passes through these four stages, which are known as *yugas*. Each of these eras is shorter than the preceding one, because morality declines more severely during each stage.

The four stages are:

- Krita-yuga
- Tetra-yuga
- Dvapara-yuga
- Kali-yuga

It is believed that we are currently in the last yuga—the *Kali Yuga* (the Dark or Iron Age), which is believed to be presided over by the Hindu goddess Kali—the goddess of darkness. As this era winds down, Hindus believe that religion will be replaced by the secularization of society. This process will culminate in the complete degeneration of humanity, and a terrible catastrophe is expected to befall mankind.

The Hindu calendar almost matches the Mayan long-count calendar that we discussed in chapter one. The Hindu Kali Yuga calendar began on February 18, 3102 BC. There is only a difference of twelve years between the beginning of Kali Yuga and the beginning of the Mayans' Fifth Great Cycle.

Both calendars began approximately five thousand years ago, and both calendars predict a totally new world or a golden age emerging in approximately five thousand years, which could be in the year 2012!

This is an amazing fact to contemplate in light of the fact that these two ancient cultures from two different hemispheres presumably had no contact with each other.

All of the events cited above, according to Hindu thinking, will be the birth pangs of a new era known as the Great Yuga, which will begin with the emergence of the Kalki Avatar. (An avatar is the incarnation of a god—a god who comes to Earth in bodily form.) People of the Bahai faith believe that

Bahaullah—the Persian founder of the Bahai faith—was this avatar.

The Hindu holy books are replete with prophetic messages. The following statements provide summaries and paraphrases of some of Hinduism's key thoughts about the future, which are found in some of the their holy books:

• Wealth will be the deciding factor of nobility during the Kali Yuga, and brute force will be used as the standard for determining if something is right or just.

• Mutual attraction will be the deciding factor in choosing a spouse, which will go against the practice of arranged marriages.

• Cheating in business will be the order of the day.

• Sexual satisfaction will be the most important thing to many.

• Unrighteousness will increase greatly.

• People will be greedy and merciless.

• Deceit, falsehood, lethargy, sleepiness, violence, grief, despondency, delusion, fear, and poverty will prevail.

• Countries will be laid waste by robbers and vagabonds.

• People's minds will be filled with anxiety and fear.

• Droughts will prevent crops from growing.

Are these statements being fulfilled in our present age? The Hindu scriptures prophesy that these conditions will be found all over the Earth prior to the end of the Kali Yuga. According to Hindus, when the deterioration of morality and righteousness is widespread, as it is today, Lord Vishnu will be born on Earth as an *avatar* who will cleanse the world of evil and re-establish righteousness and law (*dharma*).

Hindus do not truly believe in the end of the world as such, for they feel that time is cyclical. According to their belief system, this means that a new era—a new world, a new cycle, a golden age—will emerge from the ruins of our present world under the leadership of the Kalki Avatar.

ASIAN PROPHECIES FROM THE HINDUS, THE BUDDHISTS,
AND ZOROASTRIANS

However, their prophecies seem to suggest that more tribulation lies ahead for mankind before the current cycle is over. Incidentally, there are many similarities between Hindu prophecies and some of those that are found in the holy Bible.

For example, the Hindus say that their god is "the beginning and the end." This is very similar to the statement found in Revelation 22:13. In another Hindu scripture we learn about the birth of Kalki, whose mission is to destroy Koli—the equivalent of the anti-Christ. It's interesting to note that Kalki is given a white horse, which he rode upon as he conquered the world. Compare this with Revelation 19:11.

According to Hindu teaching, Kalki Avatar, the final incarnation of Vishnu, will arrive on his white horse with a sword that blazes like a comet. He will destroy the wicked and restore purity to the Earth. It is believed that continents will sink and rise at this time. Many go so far as to believe that this time has already begun or will soon arrive.

These prophecies go on to predict a major war between Kalki and China (or, perhaps, North Korea). This interpretation is based on the fact that the prophecy says that the war will be against an atheistic people. (Such people could live in either China or North Korea.) In some ways this scenario seems comparable to Judeo-Christian Scriptures about the Battle of Armageddon.

As the prophecy goes on, it seems as if Kalki and his allies will kill or injure an army that is almost twenty million strong. (The Chinese army perhaps?) This prophecy is reminiscent of something Nostradamus prophesied about the Great Wall of China. He wrote, "Before the conflict, the Great Wall will fall, the great one to death, death too sudden and lamented, born imperfect: the greater part will swim: near the river, the land stained with blood."

A prophecy from Lucia, the last living recipient of Mary's prophecy at Fatima, foretold this about China: "The events taking place in Europe are a deception. Russia will be the scourge of all nations, because it was not converted. Russia attacks the West, and China invades in Asia."

This Roman Catholic prophecy concurs with a portion of the Hindu prophecy by saying that China will try to take over all of Asia, while Russia will invade the European continent. If this prophecy comes true, the resulting conflagration could well be World War III, and, in all likelihood, it would involve the nations of Islam, as well.

Many other Hindu holy books present prophecies that are similar to the ones we have already mentioned. These scriptures include the *Ramayana*, the *Mahabarata*, and the *Vishnu Purana*.

There is a particular Hindu text that deals with eschatology (the study of the end times). It is entitled *Divya Maha Kala Jnana* (*The Divine Knowledge of Time*). It is believed that this work was written around AD 1000. It vividly describes what conditions on Earth may be like before the arrival of Kalki Avatar.

This work describes a world that is filled with sexual perversion and terrible disasters of all sorts. It gives the following descriptions and advice to those who will be (or are) alive during that (or this) time: "The leaders who will rule over the earth will be violent and will seize the goods of their subjects. The caste of servants will prevail and the outcasts will rule. Short will be their lives, insatiable their appetites; they will hardly understand the meaning of piety. Those with possessions will abandon agriculture and commerce and will live as servants or following various possessions. The leaders, with excuses of fiscal need, will rob and despoil their subjects and take away private property. Moral values and the rule of law will lessen from day to day until the world will be completely perverted and agnosticism will gain the day among men.

"The causes of devotion will be confined to physical well-being; the only bond between the sexes will be passion; the only road to success will be the lie. The earth will be honored for its material treasure only. The priestly vestments will be a substitute for the quality of the priest. A simple ablution will mean purification, the race will be incapable of producing divine birth. Men will ask: what authority have the traditional tests? Marriage will cease being a rite. Acts of devotion, however scanty, will not produce any result. Every way of life will be equally promiscuous for all. Those who own and spend more money will be the bosses of men who will have only one aim, the gaining of wealth however dishonestly. Every man will consider himself as good as a Brahmin. Men will be terrified of death and fear scarcity; by this alone they will keep up an outward appearance of religious feeling. Women will not obey the orders of their husbands or their parents. They will be selfish, abject, liars, fallen and given to evil ways. Their aims in life will be sensual satisfaction only.

"When the practices taught by the Vedas and the institutes of law shall nearly have ceased, and the close of the Kali age shall be nigh, a portion of that divine being who exists of his own spiritual nature in the character of Brahma, and who is the beginning and the end, and who comprehends all things, shall descend upon the earth. He will be born as a Kalki in the family of an eminent Brahmin of Sambhala village, endowed with the eight superhuman faculties. By his irresistible might he will destroy all the barbarians and thieves, and all whose minds are devoted to iniquity. He will then be awakened, and shall be as pellucid as crystal. The men who are thus changed by virtue of that peculiar time shall be as the seeds of human beings, and shall give birth to a race who shall follow the laws of the Krita age, the Age of Purity."[2]

Let's take a moment now to review the main points of this prophecy that predict what life will be like in the closing days of the present yuga:

• Sexual perversion will abound.

• Violent world leaders will seize the goods and the private property of their subjects.

• People's lives will be shortened, and they will be governed by their insatiable appetites.

• The knowledge of piety (dutiful and scrupulous conduct and devotion to religious duties and practices) will be gone.

• All moral values will decline, and lawlessness will increase.

• Agnosticism will increase.

• Passion will be the only bond between the sexes.

• The road to success will be paved with lies and deception.

• Marriage will no longer be considered to be a sacred rite.

• Promiscuity will rule the lives of people.

• Greed will abound.

• People will be filled with fear of death and poverty.

• Women will be selfish and will be primarily interested in sexual passion.

• The Kalki avatar will then appear, and he will destroy sinners and evil.

• A new race will emerge, and mankind will enter the Age of Purity.

In looking at this list we recognize many characteristics of our present-day society. Therefore, many believe that the fulfillment of this prophecy is taking place now and some think it will culminate in the year 2012.

I am also reminded of these words of Jesus about the end times: *"At that time many will turn away from the faith and will betray and hate each other, and many false prophets will appear and deceive many people. Because of the increase of wickedness, the love of most will grow cold"* (Matthew 24:10-12, NIV).

MAHATMA MOHANDAS GANDHI
(OCTOBER 2, 1869–JANUARY 30, 1948)

Before he was assassinated, the Indian leader Mahatma Gandhi gave a prophecy in which he predicted the future of mankind. He spoke these words to a group of his friends and colleagues: "Mankind is approaching hard times, because as soon as the measure of its sins will be full, it will be called to account by the superior power above us. You may call this event as you wish: Judgment Day, final settlement, or doomsday. It will come, most likely, very soon. Whoever will survive this settlement will see an entirely new earthly existence manifested. For a long, very long time the word 'war' will be crossed out from the dictionary of mankind, perhaps even for all time. Christmas, the festival of Christianity, will be accepted by all religions as the true festival of peace. Blessed be who will live to see this epoch!"[3]

This is a poignant prophecy of a doomsday that will be followed by a time of peace. Was Gandhi referring to the time of tribulation that will be followed by a millennium of peace that the Bible prophesies? Gandhi definitely had some knowledge of the Bible. It is said that he was attracted to Christianity, but was greatly offended by the way some Christians behaved.

Gandhi reportedly admired Jesus, and he often quoted from the Sermon on the Mount. (See Matthew 5-7.) The missionary E. Stanley Jones once asked him, "Mr. Gandhi, though you quote the words of Christ often, why is it that you appear to so adamantly reject becoming His follower?"

Gandhi answered, "Oh, I don't reject your Christ. I love your Christ. It's just that so many of you Christians are so unlike your Christ."[4]

It is said that Gandhi's feelings about Christianity were largely influenced by an incident he experienced as a young law student in South Africa. At that time he was very interested in the Christian faith. He had studied the Bible and the teachings

Mahatma Gandhi

of Jesus. He had even reached the point of contemplating becoming a Christian.

During this phase in his life, he went to a particular church. As he walked up the steps to enter the sanctuary, a white man stopped him and said, "Where do you think you're going, kaffir?" The man was rude and very condescending toward Gandhi, and he referred to the young man by way of a racial epithet.

Gandhi said, "I'd like to attend worship here."

The man replied, "There is no room for kaffirs in this church. Get out of here or I'll have my assistants throw you down the steps!"

As a result of that terrible experience, Gandhi determined not to become a member of a Christian church. Instead, he decided he would simply follow the good things he found in Christianity and the Bible.

Gandhi once asked a Christian friend, "What do you think is the essential lesson for man in the teaching of Christianity?"

The friend answered, "I could think of two or three. But one that stands out strongest is 'One is your Master Christ and all ye are brethren.'"

"Yes," replied Gandhi, "and Hinduism teaches the same great truth and Mohammedanism and Zoroastrianism, too."[5]

BUDDHIST PROPHECIES

Buddhism is the fourth largest religion in the world. There are approximately three hundred and seventy-five million Buddhists in the world today. It is the dominant religion of the Far East and is becoming increasingly popular in the Western World, as well.

Many people are attracted to Buddhism because it is a religion that promotes peace, non-violence, tolerance, morality, tranquility, and enlightenment.

Buddhism was founded during the fifth century BC by a prince from Nepal who was named Siddhartha Gautama. The name of "Buddha" means "enlightened one," hence it is possible for more than one Buddha to exist.

Siddhartha Gautama believed that his teachings would disappear after five thousand years. Others have concurred with this thought, and believe that the Buddha's teachings are disappearing on a step-by-step basis and this will go on until the Buddha is forgotten altogether.

Several sects of Buddhism have developed through the centuries. However, all would adhere to the central teachings of Buddhism, which include the Four Noble Truths:

- Life is full of suffering (*dukkha*).
- Suffering is caused by craving (*samudaya*).
- Suffering will cease only when craving ceases (*nirodha*).
- Suffering can be eliminated by following the Noble Eightfold Path.

The Noble Eightfold Path leads one to the cessation of suffering. Here are its core concepts:

- Right understanding—a proper understanding of reality.
- Right thought—thinking correctly.
- Right speech—speaking in non-hurtful, truthful, and unexaggerated ways.
- Right action—avoiding any action that might cause harm.
- Right livelihood—working in an occupation that brings good things to others and does not harm anyone.
- Right effort—individual efforts to improve one's life.
- Right mindfulness—clear consciousness.
- Right concentration—this involves deep meditation and avoids desires and cravings.

Another teaching of Buddhism involves five precepts (or five abstentions) that lead to morality and happiness. These five precepts are as follows:

• Abstain from harming all living beings—total non-violence.
• Abstain from stealing.
• Abstain from sexual misconduct in any form.
• Abstain from false speech, including lying, gossiping, etc.
• Abstain from intoxicating drinks and drugs, except for medicinal purposes.

Buddhism is a very legalistic religion that requires much of its followers. Its teachings, if followed, would undoubtedly lead to peace and happiness in the world and in individual lives. The difficulty in all of this is in knowing how to attain to such a degree of perfection. Most people, including Buddhists, I'm sure, find it exceedingly difficult to do so, because will power can only take us so far.

One concept of Buddhism involves a "Wheel of Time" (the *Kalachakra*), which goes through cycles that are similar to the Hindu concept of yugas. Buddhists believe that Buddha will become incarnate at the end of the present cycle. He will be known as Lord Maitreya (The Buddha Who Returns). This messiah-like figure is similar to the Kalki avatar of Hinduism.

Prior to his return, however, Buddhists believe that the Earth will go through major geological catastrophes that will result in complete transformations of all the continents. These changes will be so drastic that people will be able to walk from Europe to America, and all the other continents will be joined together.

When this time of upheaval and transformation is over, humanity will attain to salvation, and humanity and the gods will be delivered from their desires.

This is explained in the *Bhagavad-Gita* as follows: "Whenever there is decay of righteousness ... and there is exaltation of unrighteousness, then I Myself will come forth ... for the destruction of evil-doers, for the sake of firmly establishing righteousness, I am born from age to age."[6]

The decay of righteousness and the exaltation of unrighteousness are certainly very evident in the world today.

Gautama Buddha explained the signs that will precede the end of the age to one of his disciples. He said, "After my decease, first will occur the five disappearances. And what are the five disappearances? The disappearance of attainments [to Nirvana], the disappearance of the method [of doing so], the disappearance of [spiritual] learning, the disappearance of the symbols [of Buddhism], the disappearance of the relics....

"Then, when the dispensation of the perfect Buddha is 5,000 years old, the relics not receiving reverence and honor will go to places where they can receive them.... This ... is called the disappearance of relics."

In essence, this prophecy suggests that spiritual things will vanish as the end of the age approaches. The knowledge of Nirvana and how to experience it will completely disappear.

In a later prophecy Buddha cut the time in half, from five thousand years to twenty-five hundred years. This is explained to some degree in the Buddhist text *Abhidharmakosha*: "The monks and stream-liners will be strong in their union with Dharma for 500 years after the Blessed One's Parinirvana. In the second 500 years they will be strong in meditation; in the third period of 500 years they will be strong in erudition. In the fourth 500-year period they will only be occupied with gift-giving. The final or fifth period of 500 years will see only fighting and reproving among the monks and followers. The pure Dharma will then become invisible."[7]

Many believe that we are nearing the end of the fifth period—a time when people's sense of devotion and righteousness will no longer exist.

It is then that Maitreya (the Buddha who returns), the fully awakened one, will arrive on the scene. He is also known as the Exalted One, one who abounds in wisdom and goodness. According to the prophecy, he will be a happy and very knowledgeable teacher.

This is what Buddha himself said about Maitreya: "... the best of men, will then leave the Tushita heavens, and go for his last rebirth. As soon as he is born he will walk seven steps forward, and where he puts down his feet a jewel or a lotus will spring up. He will raise his eyes to the ten directions, and will speak these words, 'This is my last birth. There will be no birth after this one. Never will I come back here, but, all pure, I shall win Nirvana.'"[8]

Here is another prophecy about Maitreya that was put forth by Buddha: "And the Blessed One said to Ananda, I am not the first Buddha, nor shall I be the last. In due time another Buddha will arise in the world, a Holy One, a supremely enlightened one, endowed with wisdom, auspicious, embracing the universe, and incomparable leader of men, a ruler of Devas and mortals. He will reveal to you the same eternal truths, which I have taught you. He will establish his law, glorious in its spirit and in the letter. He will proclaim a righteous life wholly perfect and pure, such as I now proclaim. His disciples will number many thousands while mine number many hundreds.

"Ananda said, 'How shall we know him?'"

"The blessed one said, 'He will be known as Maitreya.'"[9]

On another occasion the Buddha prophesied about conditions on Earth when he returns: "At that time the ocean will lose much of its water, and there will be much less of it than now. In consequence a world-ruler will have no difficulties in passing across it. India, this island of Jambu, will be quite flat everywhere. It will measure ten thousand leagues, and all men will have the privilege of living on it. It will have innumerable inhabitants, who will commit no crimes or evil deeds, but will take pleasure in doing good.... Human beings are then without any blemishes, moral offenses are unknown among them, and they are full of zest and joy. Their bodies are very large and their skin has a fine hue. Their strength is quite extraordinary.

Three kinds of illness only are known—people must relieve their bowels, they must eat, they must get old....

"For 60,000 years Maitreya, the best of men, will preach the true dharma, which is compassionate towards all living beings. And when he has disciplined in his true dharma hundreds and hundreds of millions of living beings, then that leader will at last enter Nirvana. And after the great sage has entered Nirvana, his true dharma still endures for another 10,000 years...."[10]

A mystical writer from the Tibetan and Mongolian Buddhist traditions has this to say about the end of our present era: "Men will increasingly neglect their souls. The greatest corruption will reign on earth. Men will become like bloodthirsty animals, thirsting for the blood of their brothers. The crescent [a symbol of Islam] will become obscured, and its followers will descend into lies and perpetual warfare. The crowns of kings will fall.

"There will be terrible war between all the earth's peoples; entire nations will die—hunger, crimes unknown to law, formerly unthinkable to the world. The persecuted will demand the attention of the whole world. The ancient roads will be filled with multitudes going from one place to another. The greatest and most beautiful cities will perish by fire. Families will be dispersed; faith and love will disappear. The world will be emptied.

"Within fifty years there will be only three great nations. Then, within fifty years, there will be eighteen years of war and cataclysms."[11]

The following passage is from "The Legend of the Great Stupa," which was believed to be written by Padma Sambhava, the man who brought Buddhism to Tibet: "As the Kali yuga progresses towards the final conflagration, life expectancy of man decreases and the weight of darkness becomes more intense, but these remain restraints on the downward path when the Voice of Buddha is heard and the

Path of Dharma followed. Towards the end of the era, when the duration of a man's life span has been reduced from sixty to fifty years and there has been no respite in man's increasing egoism, these conditions will prevail,... householders fill the monasteries and there is fighting before the altar; the temples are used as slaughterhouses. The ascetics of the caves return to the cultivated valleys.... Priests and spiritual leaders turn to robbery, brigandage and thievery. Disorder becomes chaos, turning to panic which rages like wildfire. Corrupt and selfish men become leaders....

"When religious duties are forgotten, spirits of darkness, which had been controlled by ritual power, become unloosed and frenzied and govern the mind of whatever they possess. Spirits of vindictive power possess monks;... enchanting spirits causing disease possess men; grasping, quarreling spirits possess women; spirits of wantonness possess maidens; spirits of depravity possess nuns; spirits of rebellion and malice possess children; every man, woman, and child in the country becomes possessed by uncontrollable forces of darkness....

"Men become lewd and licentious; women become unchaste; monks ignore their discipline and moral code....

"The celestial order, disrupted, loosens plague, famine and war to terrorize terrestrial life. The planets run wild, and the stars fall out of their constellations, great burning stars arise, bringing unprecedented disaster. No rain falls in season, but out of season; the valleys are flooded. Famine, frost and hail govern many unproductive years."[12]

This is certainly a very dreadful picture of what the end times may be like. When catastrophes and tragedies of this dimension begin to occur, it is certain that human beings will become vicious in their desire to survive. People will begin to blame others for their problems and to seek vengeance in whatever ways they can. The best we can hope for as a result of this Buddhist prophecy is that people will awaken to the true values of honesty, compassion, and spirituality.

Precise time lines are not provided in these prophecies, but every indication is that they could well be referring to sometime in the not-too-distant future.

A PROPHECY FROM THE 13TH DALAI LAMA

The thirteenth Dalai Lama predicted the invasion of Tibet and announced that he would die early. His name was Thubten Gyatso (February 12, 1876-December 17, 1933). Here are his words: "Very soon in this land (with a harmonious blend of religion and politics) deceptive acts may occur from without and within. At that time, if we do not dare to protect our territory, our spiritual personalities ... may be exterminated without trace, the property and authority of our Lakangs [residences of reincarnated lamas] and monks may be taken away. Moreover, our political system, developed by the Three Great Dharma Kings ... will vanish without anything remaining. The property of all people, high and low, will be seized and the people forced to become slaves. All living beings will have to endure endless days of suffering and will be stricken with fear. Such a time will come."[13]

Such a time has come for the people of Tibet, and perhaps similar things will happen to people around the world, as many other prophecies predict, including those of the Zoroastrians, which are discussed in the next sections of this chapter.

ZOROASTRIAN PROPHECIES

Zoroastrianism is a religion and philosophy that is based on the teachings of a prophet named Zoroaster, who was a religious reformer of ancient Persia (now Iran). This religion presents the oldest eschatology (study of the end times) in recorded history. Zoroaster lived from 628 BC to 551 BC. It is said that he experienced a religious vision when he was thirty years old, and, as a result, he spent the next ten years traveling and preaching throughout Persia.

Zoroastrianism is believed to be the oldest of the monotheistic creedal religions and has had a great influence on mankind through the centuries. Zoroastrians believe that good and evil are separate entities that are at war with each other. The holy book of Zoroastrianism is the *Avesta*, which is filled partly with Zoroaster's hymns, sacred writings, and prayers and the writings of several others.

From the following quotations that are attributed to Zoroaster we can learn a great deal about his philosophy and the teachings of Zoroastrianism:

- "When you doubt, abstain."
- "Doing good to others is not a duty, it is a joy, for it increases our own health and happiness."
- "Be good, be kind, be humane, and charitable; love your fellows; console the afflicted; pardon those who have done you wrong."
- Suffer no anxiety, for he who is a sufferer of anxiety does not regard the enjoyment of the world and the spirit, and contraction happens to his body and soul."

The basic beliefs of Zoroastrianism include the following:

- There is one universal and transcendent God (Ahura Mazda). All worship should be directed toward him. Ahura Mazda is the beginning and the end, the creator of everything which can and cannot be seen.
- Ahura Mazda's creation is the antithesis of chaos, falsehood, and disorder.
- One should live life with good thoughts, good words, and good deeds. (These are individual, free-will choices.)
- Ahura Mazda will ultimately prevail over Angra Mainyu/ Ahriman (the malevolent enemy). When this happens, the universe will undergo a cosmic renovation and time will end.
- The Earth will end by fire sent from above.
- At the end of time a savior-type figure will appear and will bring about a final renovation of the world. This is when the dead will be revived.

• In the end times evil will be purged from the Earth (through a tidal wave of molten metal). This will come about from the heavens through a cosmic battle that will involve spiritual forces.

• At the end of the battle between the righteous and the wicked, the Final Judgment of humanity will begin. (Sinners will be punished for only three days, after which they will be forgiven.)

• Water and fire are agents of ritual purity.

• The spiritual law of Zoroastrianism is known as *daena*. This term is used to mean religion, faith, law, and even dharma, the Hindu concept of duty.

• Good transpires for those who do righteous deeds; those who do evil can only blame themselves for their eventual ruin.

Zoroastrians believe in cosmic cycles that last twelve thousand years each. Each of these cycles is divided into three-thousand-year-long epochs. Currently we are in the second epoch, which is known as the "Time of Mixture."

Adherents of Zoroastrianism are awaiting the birth of a savior. They feel that his advent is overdue. It is believed that when Zoroaster died, his sperm was miraculously preserved in Iran's Lake Kansaoya. According to their belief, at some point in the future a girl who swims in the lake will be impregnated by Zoroaster's sperm.[14]

They say that this young lady will give birth to three sons, each of whom will have a role that will lead people into righteousness.

Here are some excerpts from a prophecy about the end times that comes from the Zoroastian text, *Zand-i Vohuman Yasht:*

"… the most evil period is coming … a myriad of kinds of demons with disheveled hair, of the race of wrath, rush into the country of Iran from the direction of the east, which has an inferior race and race of wrath.…"

"They have uplifted banners, they slay those living in the world, they have their hair disheveled on the back, and they are mostly a small and inferior race,...

"Through witchcraft they rush into these countries of Iran which I ... created, since they burn and damage many things; and the house of the house owner, the land of the land-digger, prosperity, nobility, sovereignty, religion, truth, agreement, security, enjoyment, and every characteristic which I, Ohrmazd, created ... and the direst destruction and trouble will come into notice.

"... They will lead these Iranian countries of Ohrmazd into a desire for evil, into tyranny and misgovernment [could this be a depiction of present-day Iran?], those demons with disheveled hair who are deceivers, so that what they say they do not do, and they are of a vile religion, so that what they do not say they do.

"And their assistance and promise have no sincerity, there is no law, they preserve no security, and on the support they provide no one relies; with deceit, rapacity, and misgovernment they will devastate these, my Iranian cousins....

"All men will become deceivers, great friends will become of different parties, and respect, affection, hope, and regard for the soul will depart from the world; the affection of the father will depart from the son; and that of the brother from his brother; the son-in-law will become a beggar from his father-in-law, and the mother will be parted and estranged from the daughter.

"... the sun is more unseen and more spotted; the year, month, and day are shorter; and the earth ... is more barren, and fuller of highwaymen; and the crop will not yield the seed, so that of the crop of the corn fields in ten cases, seven will diminish and three will increase, and that which increases does not become ripe; and vegetation, trees, and shrubs will diminish; when one shall take a hundred, ninety will diminish

ZOROASTRIAN SCRIPTURES PREDICT THAT
A COMET WILL DESTROY THE EARTH.

and ten will increase, and that which increases gives no pleasure and flavor....

"And all the world will be burying and clothing the dead, and burying the dead and washing the dead will be by law; the burning, bringing to water and fire, and eating of dead matter they practice by law and do not abstain from....

"And a dark cloud makes the whole sky night, and the hot wind and the cold wind arrive, and bring along fruit and seed of corn, even the rain in its proper time; and it does not rain, and that which rains also rains more noxious creatures than water; and the water of rivers and springs will diminish, and there will be no more increase....

"The sun and the moon show signs, and the moon becomes manifest of various colors; earthquakes, too, become numerous, and the wind comes more violently; in the world want, distress, and discomfort come more into view...."[15]

One of the Zoroastrian scriptures predicts that a comet will destroy the Earth. The comet is called Gochihr. Its "fire and halo" will be so intense, according to this prophecy, that all metals and minerals will ignite and burn up the world. A boiling flood of metal will flow all over the Earth. All the righteous (and the wicked souls that will be released from hell) will have to pass through this molten river. As they do so, the wicked will be purified of their sins via the fire, but to the righteous ones it will seem as if they are simply passing through warm milk.

The following are some other Zoroastrian prophecies:

• Seven ages will occur—the golden age, the silver age, the copper age, the brass age, the lead age, the steel age, and the iron age.

• When the winter of the tenth century arrives, crops will cease to yield seed, plants will be stunted, and people will become tiny and listless.

• Everyone will worship greed and false religions. They will suffer from hunger of soul.

- Clouds and fog will make the sky dark.
- Hot and cold winds will carry away fruits and grain.
- Rain will not fall during its usual seasons.

The Asian prophecies we have discussed in this chapter give us many insights into the human condition and what is likely to happen to mankind, if people do not learn to worship God in spirit and truth and to cooperate with one another in love, honesty, and compassion.

They indicate that the sins of mankind need to be purged from the human heart and from the Earth. During the Middle Ages the Roman Catholic Church put forth a list of the Seven Deadly Sins, and these particular sins are discussed in the prophecies of Hinduism, Buddhism, and Zorastrianism, as well.

The Seven Deadly Sins are greed, lust, envy, pride, wrath, gluttony, and sloth. According to the church's teachings and many Asian prophecies, they need to be replaced by the Seven Cardinal Virtues, which are faith, hope, love, prudence, justice, temperance, and fortitude.

Teilhard de Chardin (May 1, 1881-April 10, 1955), a French Jesuit, who was a paleontologist, biologist, and philosopher, wrote, "Someday, after mastering the winds, the waves, the tides and gravity, we shall harness for God the energies of love, and then, for a second time in the history of the world, man will have discovered fire."

He also said, "We are not human beings having a spiritual experience. We are spiritual beings having a human experience."

There is a direct connection between his wise insights and those of the Asians, which are found within this chapter's prophecies. Each of us would be well advised to take these thoughts into consideration and apply them to our lives.

ENDNOTES

1. *Hindu Prophecies.* http://www.bci.org/prophecy-fulfilled/hindusa.htm
2. Ibid.
3. *Prophecy: a History of the Future.* http://www.rexresearch.com/prophist/phf6asia.htm
4. Ibid.
5. *Gandhi and Christianity.* http://www.kamat.com/mmgandhi/chrisitan.htm
6. *Prophecy: a History of the Future.* http://www.rexresearch.com/prophist/phf6asia.htm
7. Ibid.
8. Ibid.
9. Ibid.
10. Ibid.
11. Ibid.
12. *Buddhist Prophecy.* http://www.reversespins.com/buddhistprophecy.html
13. Ibid.
14. *Zoroastrian Prophecies.* http://www.avesta.org/zcomet.html
15. *Prophecy: a History of the Future.* http://www.rexresearch.com/prophist/phf6asia.htm

Other Resources That Were Consulted in the Preparation of This Chapter

1. *Hindu Prophecies: the Kalki Purana.* http://ww-iii.tripod.com/hindu.htm
2. *Prophecies of the Ages.* http://www.dayofgod.net/hindu/main.htm
3. *Zoroastrianism.* http://en.wikipedia.org/wiki/Zoroastrianism
4. *Zoroaster.* http://www.answers.com/topic/Zoroaster

Additional Resources You May Wish to Explore

1. *World Religions in a Nutshell* by Ray Comfort. Published by Bridge-Logos, Alachua, Florida, 2008.

2. *The History of Zoroastrianism* by Mary Boyce. Published by Brill, 1996.

3. *Encyclopedia of American Religions* by Gordon J. Melton. Published by Gale Research, Detroit, 1996.

4. *The Dawn and Twilight of Zoroastrianism* by Robert Charles Zaehner. Published by Phoenix Press, London, 1961.

11

THE DAY OF THE LORD AND HEBREW PROPHECIES

*Blow ye the trumpet in Zion, and sound an alarm in my
holy mountain: let all the inhabitants of the land tremble:
for the day of the Lord cometh, for it is nigh at hand. A day
of darkness and of gloominess, a day of clouds and thick
darkness, as the morning spread upon the mountains.... They
shall run to and fro in the city; they shall run upon the wall,
they shall climb up upon the houses; they shall enter in at the
windows like a thief. The earth shall quake before them; the
heavens shall tremble: the sun and the moon shall be dark,
and the stars shall withdraw their shining: and the Lord shall
utter his voice before his army: for his camp is very great:
for he is strong that executeth his word: for the day of the
Lord is great and very terrible; and who can abide it?*
JOEL 2:1-2; 2:9-11, KJV

JUDAISM

Judaism is a monotheistic religion that is based on the
Scriptures (referred to as the Old Testament by Christians)
and the Talmud, a collection of writings that present Jewish
civil and religious laws. The Talmud is divided into two parts:
the *Mishnah* (the text) and the *Gemara* (a commentary on the
text).

There are four major sects within Judaism:

1. Orthodox Judaism—The followers of Orthodox Judaism believe in a strict, legalistic interpretation of the Scriptures and the Talmud. They believe that the Messiah will arise out of the lineage of David. Some within the Orthodox community believe that this era will conclude with many supernatural events taking place, including a bodily resurrection of the dead.

2. Conservative Judaism—Many conservative Jews believe in a Messianic Era that is yet to come. Emet ve-Emunah writes, "We do not know when the Messiah will come, nor whether he will be a charismatic human figure or is a symbol of the redemption of mankind from the evils of the world. Through the doctrine of a Messianic figure, Judaism teaches that every individual being must live as if he or she, individually, has the responsibility to bring about the messianic age. Beyond that, we echo the words of Maimonides based on the prophet Habakkuk (2:3) that though he may tarry, yet do we wait for him each day" (From *Statement of Principles of Conservative Judaism*.)[1]

The full text of Habakkuk 2:3 says, "For the revelation awaits an appointed time; it speaks of the end and will not be proved false. Though it linger, wait for it; it will certainly come and will not delay" (NIV).

3. Reform Judaism—This group tends to be a bit more liberal in theology and interpretation than either Orthodox or Conservative Judaism. Reform Jews believe that a future Messianic Era will come, but they appear to be less certain about a personal Messiah being a part of it.

The prayers of Reform Judaism refer to "redemption" rather than a "Redeemer," as such. They have also removed prayers for the restoration of the House of David.

4. Reconstructionist Judaism—Reconstructionist Jews reject the idea of a personal Messiah and a Messianic Age altogether. However, they do believe that human beings can work together to improve this world (reconstructionism).

THE DAY OF THE LORD AND HEBREW PROPHECIES

The philosophy of this branch of Judaism is quite similar to humanism. Their prayers no longer reflect a belief in a personal Messiah.

There are approximately fourteen million Jews in the world today. Nearly six million of them live in the United States, and approximately five million live in Israel. The rest are scattered around the world. In addition to the sects of Judaism that I've listed above, there is another relatively large group—atheistic Jews. In fact, recent statistics suggest that only 30 percent of Jews are "absolutely certain" that God exists, while 12 percent believe there is no God.[2]

There are observant Jews, secular Jews, agnostic Jews, and even atheist Jews! So, as you can see, it is hard to define a Jew in terms of specific matters of theology and a worldview that applies to them all.

MAIMONIDES (1135-1204) AND THE END OF DAYS

Moses Maimondes (aka Rabbi Moses ben Maimon) was a Spanish philosopher, physician, and rabbi, who is considered to be one of the greatest Torah scholars of all time. The Torah can be either the whole body of Jewish religious literature, including the Scriptures and the Talmud, or it may simply refer to the Pentateuch—the first five books in the Bible that were written by Moses.

One of the best-known quotations attributed to Maimonides is: "Give a man a fish and you feed him for a day; teach a man to fish and you feed him for a lifetime." He also gave this practical advice, "Anticipate charity by preventing poverty; assist the reduced fellow man, either by a considerate gift or a sum of money or by teaching him a trade or by putting him in the way of business so that he may earn an honest livelihood and not be forced to the dreadful alternative of holding out his hand for charity. This is the highest step and summit of charity's golden ladder."[3]

Maimonides' philosophical admonitions are applicable to daily living. He also taught about the end times (the End of Days—the Day of the Lord), phrases that refer to the Messianic Era. He believed that the Messiah will redeem Israel in the End of Days.

WHEN WILL THE MESSIAH COME?

Jews anticipate the arrival of the Messiah every day, and they pray that God will usher in the Messianic Era. It is even reported that some Jews, who were prisoners in Nazi concentration camps, would sing, *"Ani Maamin"* ("I believe in the coming of Mashiach [the Messiah]" as they stood in the lines leading to the gas chambers.[4]

According to the Talmud, the time for the Messiah's coming has been predestined. Many believe that meritorious behavior will hasten his appearing. The "end of time," according to Talmudic scholars, will take place before the Hebrew year 6000, which would be the year 2240 according to the Gregorian calendar. (That is a little over two hundred years from now.) It is important to realize that some Jews believe it could happen before that, depending on how people live.

Many Torah authorities believe that the Messiah will come very soon. In fact, the Lubavitcher Rebbe has stated that Messianic redemption is imminent. Incidentally, many Jews believe that the Messiah will be a direct descendant of King David, and he must be very knowledgeable in Torah learning. Many men in our present day could well qualify for this, particularly those who descend from the Chief Rabbi of Prague in the sixth century—Rabbi Yehuda Loew—who is known as the *Maharal*, for he is a direct descendant of King David.

Maimonides said that when we recognize a human being who possesses the necessary qualities to be the Messiah, we may presume that he is, indeed, the Messiah. This, of course, would be particularly true if that individual rebuilds the Temple in Jerusalem.

It is believed by many that when the Temple is rebuilt, Jews from all over the world will gather in Israel to worship the Lord, a fulfillment of this Scripture: "*But in the last days it shall come to pass, that the mountain of the house of the Lord shall be established in the top of the mountains, and it shall be exalted above the hills; and people shall flow into it. And many nations shall come, and say, Come, and let us go up to the mountain of the Lord, and to the house of the God of Jacob; and he will teach us of his ways, and we will walk in his paths: for the law shall go forth of Zion, and the word of the Lord from Jerusalem*" (Micah 4:1-2, KJV).

Maimonides goes on to say that the Sanhedrin (the highest court and council of the Jewish nation) will be reestablished in order to rule over all matters of law, both religious and civil. At this time, also, it is believed that Jews will return to the full observance of the Torah. There is evidence to suggest that this latter prediction is being fulfilled in our present day, as Jews return to their sacred roots, learn Hebrew, and study the Scriptures.

Some believe that God himself will rebuild the Temple. Others believe that it will be rebuilt by the Messiah. Still others think it will be a combination of the two.

Many Jews generally accept the idea that the Messianic Era will be a time of miracles, signs, and wonders. Some think there are actually two Messianic Eras—according to them, the first would be a period in which there will be no miracles, followed by an era in which the miraculous will become relatively commonplace.

Maimonides writes, "Neither the order of the occurrence of these events nor their precise detail is among the fundamental principles of the faith ... one should wait and believe in the general conception of the matter."

A New World Order

What will happen during the Messianic Era? According to many Jews, the nations of the world will endeavor to work together under a new world order after the Messiah comes. When this happens, there will be no more wars or conflicts. Negativity in all its forms will cease, and it will be replaced by love, goodness, kindness, and peace.

People will be prosperous and healthy during this era, as well, and everyone will be pursuing a fuller knowledge of God. There will be less materialism, because people will be primarily focused on spiritual matters.

Prior to this Golden Age, however, there will be great tribulation, travail, and turmoil. It is predicted that there will be a world recession (perhaps even worse than the present one), and cruel dictators will be in control of many governments.

Traditional Jewish teaching suggests that a great war will take place, as well. This is known to many as the War of Gog and Magog.

Some believe that Elijah will return to announce the coming of the Messiah. There are others, however, that believe the Messiah will arrive on the scene without any announcement whatsoever.

The Kabbala

Kabbala writings are very esoteric and some open a window to the future. The most important of the Kabbalistic texts is known as the Zohar. It is believed that this text explains everything about the universe. Some Jews believe that the Zohar contains secrets that will unlock encoded messages within the Scriptures.

Some of these encoded messages are reported to be prophecies about Israel's future. One of the prophecies is interpreted as saying that enemies of Israel will attack the Holy Land during the night with major chemical and biological warfare. It goes on to say that Israel will respond with nuclear weapons, and this use of nuclear weapons will usher in the end of the world.

The prophecy proceeds to describe a world war of unprecedented proportions, and New York City will be hit by nuclear weapons. All of this horror will be preceded by major changes in the Earth, which will include volcanic activity, earthquakes, massive storms of all kinds, and a time of cold and darkness that will last at least fifteen days.[5]

During this time miracles, according to the Kabbala, will become commonplace. Devout men will be able to heal the sick and prevent natural disasters. They will be like Moses, who was instrumental in the parting of the Red Sea.

The sacred text goes on to say that a ball of fire will come from the heavens and hit the Earth. This, according to the prophecy, will block the light of the sun for several days, and people will forget about the sun altogether.

One of the futuristic writings of the Kabbala states that only seven thousand righteous men will be found in Israel in the end times. Kabbalistic writings say that all of these end-times events will occur sometime after the year 2006.[6]

THE DAY OF THE LORD

What is the meaning of "the Day of the Lord"? This is a phrase that appears in many Jewish prophecies about the end times. Essentially, it refers to a period (not necessarily a twenty-four-hour day) at the end of time. It will be a time of great darkness, especially for those who are not living for the Lord. It is also known as "the end of days" (*aharit ha-yamim*).

This is when the Messiah will come and cleanse the Earth. It will be a time of judgment and a time of restoration, as well, as we've mentioned above.

In addition to the passage from Joel that is quoted in the epigraph at the beginning of this chapter, there are several other Old Testament Scriptures that deal with the Day of the Lord. These passages describe what the prophets of the Old Testament and many modern Jews think will happen in the end times:

- *"The Lord Almighty has a day in store for all the proud and lofty, for all that is exalted (and they will be humbled).... The arrogance of man will be brought low and the pride of men humbled; the Lord alone will be exalted in that day, and the idols will totally disappear."* (Isaiah 2:12-18, NIV)

- *"Men will flee to caves in the rocks and to holes in the ground from dread of the Lord and the splendor of his majesty when he rises to shake the earth.... Stop trusting in man, who has but a breath in his nostrils."* (Isaiah 2:19-22, NIV)

- *"Wail, for the day of the Lord is near; it will come like destruction from the Almighty. Because of this, all hands will go limp, every man's heart will melt. Terror will seize them, pain and anguish will grip them; they will writhe like a woman in labor. They will look aghast at each other, their faces aflame. See, the day of the Lord is coming—a cruel day, with wrath and fierce anger—to make the land desolate and destroy the sinners within it."* (Isaiah 13:6-9, NIV)

- *"The stars of heaven and their constellations will not show their light. The rising sun will be darkened and the moon will not give its light. I will punish the world for its evil, the wicked for their sins. I will put an end to the arrogance of the haughty and will humble the pride of the ruthless.... Therefore I will make the heavens tremble; and the earth will shake from its place at the wrath of the Lord Almighty, in the day of his burning anger."* (Isaiah 13:10-13, NIV)

These are only a few of the passages that reveal that the Hebrew concept of the Day of the Lord refers to a dreadful and terrifying time. It will be a time when God's anger will be unleashed upon those who are haughty and proud. God will shake the Earth, and people will attempt to flee from Him and His wrath. The land will become desolate and the celestial bodies—the sun, the moon, and the stars—will stop giving light. Great fear and terror will fill human hearts everywhere. These things will precede the coming of the Messiah.

A PROPHETIC RELIGION

A quick scan of the Hebrew Scriptures, including ones I've already cited, leads one to realize that Judaism is a very prophetic religion. Prophecies of various kinds are found throughout the books of the Old Testament.

The word *prophecy* can refer to a revelation or foretelling of the future; it can also simply mean speaking forth the Word of God. For example, a prophet might speak to a leader, warning him that God expects him to live and rule in righteousness, or a prophet might speak to the people in order to exhort them to obey the Law. On the other hand, a prophet might speak to either an individual or a group to let them know what God has revealed to him about the future and how it will affect their lives.

The Hebrew word for prophet (*nahbi*) stems from the verb *nibba*, which means "to make an announcement." Prophets make announcements to the people and their leaders on behalf of God. Sometimes these announcements are words of encouragement, but very frequently they are warnings and dire predictions of divine judgment.

HEBREW ESCHATOLOGY

In this chapter we have already covered several major points related to Hebrew eschatology—the study and conclusions about the end times from a Jewish perspective.

The following list sums up some of the main points of Hebrew eschatology, including some we have not discussed previously, and certain Scriptures associated with them. Many, but not all Jews believe these things will take place in the end times. I have simply listed them here in random fashion, and I have not attempted to develop their chronology:

- Jews will return to the Torah and learn its principles. (See Jeremiah 31:33.)
- Jews will return to Israel from the four corners of the Earth. (Since 1948, this return of Jews to the Holy Land continues; see Isaiah 11:12.)
- The "man of sin" and "the abomination of desolation" shall be revealed. (See Daniel 12:11.)
- People will flee to the valley of the mountains. (See Zechariah 14:5.)
- A time of great tribulation will take place. This very frightening era is described in the Book of Daniel, as follows: *"At that time Michael, the great prince who protects your people, will arise. There will be a time of distress such as has not happened from the beginning of nations until then"* (Daniel 12:1).
- The sun, the moon, and the stars will be darkened. (See Joel 2:10.)
- The Temple will be rebuilt in Jerusalem. (See Daniel 11:45 and Ezekiel 40.)
- The Sanhedrin will be reestablished. (See Isaiah 1:26.)
- The Messiah—a descendant of David—will come, the great *shofar* (ram's horn) will be blown, and the voice of the archangel shall sound. (See Isaiah 27:12-13.)
- People of the world will look to the Messiah (the King) for guidance. (See Isaiah 2:4.)
- The world will worship the one true God. (See Isaiah 2:17.)
- Evil and tyranny will not be able to continue under the rule of the Messiah. (See Isaiah 11:4.)

- People will be resurrected from the dead. (See Daniel 12:2 and Isaiah 26:19.)
- Death will be "swallowed up" and this will last forever. (See Isaiah 25:8.)
- The wrath of the Messiah will be poured forth. (See Zechariah 14:3.)
- The knowledge of God will fill the world. (See Isaiah 11:9.)
- Jews will experience eternal joy and gladness. (See Isaiah 51:11.)
- Nations will understand and acknowledge the crimes they committed against Israel. (See Isaiah 52:13-53:5.)
- Gentiles will turn to the Jews for instruction and guidance. (See Zechariah 8:23.)
- Ruined cities of Israel will be rebuilt. (See Ezekiel 36:35.)
- The weapons of war will be destroyed. (See Ezekiel 39:9.)

All these points give us a good overview of the Jewish concept of the end times. As you can see, many of these things have already taken place. However, the Temple has yet to be rebuilt, but it is possible that this could happen miraculously without human intervention, according to some.

THE MESSIANIC AGE

Maimonides wrote, "The Messianic age is when the Jews will regain their independence and all return to the land of Israel. The Messiah will be a very great king, he will achieve great fame, and his reputation among the Gentile nations will be even greater than King Solomon. His great righteousness and the wonders that he will bring about will cause all peoples to make peace with him and all lands to serve him....

"Nothing will change in the Messianic age, however, except that Jews will regain their independence. Rich and poor, strong and weak, will still exist. However, it will be very easy for people to make a living, and with very little effort they will be able to accomplish much.... It will be a time when the number of wise men will increase ... war shall not exist, and nation shall no longer lift up sword against nation....

"The Messianic age will be highlighted by a community of the righteous and dominated by goodness and wisdom. It will be ruled by the Messiah, a righteous and honest king, outstanding in wisdom, and close to God. Do not think that the ways of the world or the laws of nature will change, this is not true. The world will continue as it is. The prophet Isaiah predicted, 'The wolf shall live with the sheep, the leopard shall lie down with the kid.' This, however, is merely allegory, meaning that the Jews will live safely, even with the formerly wicked nations....

"All nations will return to the true religion and will no longer steal or oppress.... Our sages and prophets did not long for the Messianic age in order that they might rule the world and dominate the Gentiles.... The only thing they wanted was to be free for Jews to involve themselves with the Torah and its wisdom." (From Maimonides' tractate Sanhedrin of the Babylonian Talmud).[7]

Maimonides' picture of life during the Messianic Era is very compelling and desirable. Bear in mind, however, that, according to Hebrew prophecy, it will be preceded by great trials and tribulations for the human race.

The end of the world, according to Judaism, is called the *acharit hayamim*, and this involves the overturning of the old world order and the creation of a new world order in which Almighty God is recognized as "the God of Abraham, Isaac, and Jacob."

The new world order envisioned by these prophets will be built upon this foundation: *"Hear, O Israel: The Lord our God, the Lord is one"* (Deuteronomy 6:4, KJV).

One Jewish sage wrote, "Let the end of days come, but may I not live to see them." (He obviously did not want to go through the conflict and suffering that will precede the Messianic Era, which is described by the Prophet Malachi in the next section of this chapter.)

THE PROPHET MALACHI

The last chapter of the final book in the Old Testament (Malachi 4) deals with the Day of the Lord. The Prophet Malachi puts forth this reminder to Jewish people: *"'Surely the day is coming; it will burn like a furnace. All the arrogant and every evildoer will be stubble, and that day that is coming will set them on fire,' says the Lord Almighty. 'Not a root or a branch will be left to them. But for you who revere my name, the sun of righteousness will rise with healing in its wings. And you will go out and leap like calves released from the stall. Then you will trample down the wicked; they will be ashes under the soles of your feet on the day when I do these things,' says the Lord Almighty.*

"'Remember the law of my servant Moses, the decrees and laws I gave him at Horeb for all Israel.

"'See, I will send you the prophet Elijah before that great and dreadful day of the Lord comes. He will turn the hearts of the fathers to their children, and the hearts of the children to their fathers; or else I will come and strike the land with a curse'" (NIV).

ENDNOTES

1. *Evet ve-Emunah. Statement of Principles of Conservative Judaism.* www.scribd.com/doc/3491343/emet-veemunah-statement-of-principles-of-conservative-judaism
2. Comfort, Ray, *World Religions in a Nutshell*, 2008, Bridge-Logos Publishers, Alachua, Florida.

3. http://222.brainyquote.com/quotes/quotes/m/maimonides143974.html

4. *Ani Maamin—I Believe.* www.road90.com/watch.php?id=34-44k

5. *Prophecies of 2012.* http://comingglobalwarwithufos.com/Predictions%20by%20all%20body.htm

6. Ibid.

7. Jewish Eschatology. http://www.apocalypse-soon.com/jewish_eschatology.htm

Other Resources That Were Consulted in the Preparation of This Chapter

1. *The Latter Days.* http://magog.web-site.co.il/gog/e_main.shtml

2. *Abomination of Desolation.* http://en.wikipedia.org/wiki/Abomination_of_desolation

3. *The Abomination of Desolation.* http://www.whitehorsemedia.com/articles/details.cfm?art=58

4. *Daniel Chapter 12.* http://ncbible.org/resources/DanielComm12.html

5. *What Is the Jewish Belief About "The End of Days"?* http://www.noahide.org/articl.asp?Level=391&Parent=90

6. *Messianic Jewish Eschatology.* http://www.messianic.com/articles/eschatology.htm

7. *Prophecy—Hebrew Prophecy.* http://science.jrank.org/pages/10880/Prophecy-Hebrew-Prophecy.html

8. *Jewish Eschatology.* http://en.wikipedia.org/wiki/Jewish_eschatology

9. *Maimonides.* http://en.wikipedia.org/wiki/Maimonides

Additional Resources You May Wish to Explore

1. AskMoses.com

2. Sanders, E.P. "Paul and Palestinian Judaism." Fortress Press.

3. Wright, N.T. "The New Testament and the People of God." Fortress Press: 1992.

4. *The Message of Daniel* by Ronald S. Wallace. Inter-varsity Press, 1979.

5. *Maimonides' Principles: the Fundamentals of Jewish Faith,* in "The Aryeh Kaplan Anthology, Volume 1," Mesorah Publications, 1994.

6. *A History of Jewish Philosophy* by Isaac Husik, Dover Publiscations, Inc. 2002.

12

THE MAHDI AND END-TIME PROPHECIES OF ISLAM

When Daniel specified the period between its distress and relief, between the era of anguish and the era of blessing, he put as forty-five years! We have already seen that he specified the time of the establishment of the abomination of desolation as the year 1967, which is what in fact occurred. Therefore, the end—or the beginning of the end—will be 1967+45=2012.[1]

SAFAR IBN ABD AL-RAHMAN AL-HAWALI

Allah's messenger (may peace be upon him) came to us all of a sudden as we were (busy in discussion). He said: "What do you discuss about?" They (the companions) said, "We are discussing about the Last Hour." Thereupon he said, "It will not come until you see ten signs before" and (in this connection) he made a mention of the smoke, Dajjal [the imposter—an anti-Christ figure], the beast, the rising of the sun from the West, the descent of Jesus, Son of Mary (Allah be pleased with him), the Gog and Magog, and land-slidings in three places, one in the East, one in the West, and one in Arabia at the end of which fire would burn forth from the Yemen, and would drive people to the place of their assembly.[2]

SAHIH MUSLIM BOOK 041, NUMBER 6931

THE ISLAMIC RELIGION

Islam is the world's second-largest religion, with approximately 1.5 billion followers. (This means that one in every five people in the world is a Muslim.) It is one of the youngest of the leading world religions, and it appears to be the fastest growing of them all. It is believed that Islam could become the world's largest religion by the middle of this century.

The founder of Islam was Muhammad, who said that he was visited by the angel Gabriel while he was meditating inside a cave. He reported that his relationship with this angel went on for twenty-three years, during which time he received numerous messages, which he eventually recorded.

The presumed-to-be angelic teachings Muhammad received have formed the basis for Islam, a word that means "submission." Muslims believe that Islam was the first and original religion. They also teach that Jesus was one of a long list of prophets, and Muhammad was the last of these prophets.

After the death of Muhammad, Muslims could not agree about who his successor should be. A schism then occurred, and they divided into two main groups: the Sunnis and the Shi'ites. Approximately 85 percent of Muslims are Sunnis, and approximately 15 percent are Shi'ites.

The holy book of Islam is the Koran (or Qur'an). Muhammad transcribed the angelic messages he received, but they were not formed into a book (the Koran) until after his death. This sacred text is divided into 114 chapters that are known as Suras, and they cover a variety of topics, including theology, law, history, ethics, etc.

Islam teaches about five articles of faith, or dedications and principles, which are:

1. Belief in one God (Allah), and his attributes are revealed in his "ninety-nine most beautiful names." Belief that Allah is the creation and creator of all, including the prophets.

2. Belief in the four archangels and numerous other angels, who must obey Allah. There are other supernatural creatures known as *jinn*, as well. (Some of these entities are considered to be good and some are considered to be bad—evil spirits.)

3. Belief in the four main Scriptures of Islam: the Pentateuch (the first five books in the Bible), the Psalms, the gospel, and the Koran. This includes belief in the divine inspiration of all these Scriptures.

4. Belief in twenty-eight apostles, who are the prophets of Islam. The six greatest apostles/prophets are Adam, Noah, Abraham, Moses, Jesus, and Muhammad. A Muslim must respect and follow the laws that were put forth by these men.

5. Belief in the Day of Judgment, which will take place during the last days. It is a time when everyone will have to answer to Allah, and everyone will be judged according to what they have done.

THE FIVE PILLARS OF ISLAM

The Five Pillars of Islam, which are listed below, are rules that Muslims are expected to follow. The behavior of a Muslim is expected to conform to these five precepts:

1. A Muslim must declare openly and publicly that there is no other god than Allah.

2. A Muslim must pray at least five times daily. These prayers follow the procession of the sun—a pre-dawn prayer, a prayer at noon, an afternoon prayer, a prayer at dusk, and a bedtime prayer. Prayers at other times are optional, not mandatory.

3. A Muslim must give at least 2.5 percent of his or her investments and savings to Islam. (These offerings are to be used to help the needy.)

4. During the holy month of Ramadan (the ninth month of the Islamic calendar, the month in which it is believed that the Koran was revealed to Muhammad), a Muslim must fast

every day. (This means that no food is to be consumed between dawn and dusk.)

5. Every Muslim must make a *hajj* (a pilgrimage to Mecca—where Muhammad was born) at least once in his or her lifetime.

According to many Islamic teachings, Muslims should practice kindness toward others with a charitable heart. They believe that Allah said that a Muslim is a person from whose hands and tongue others are safe.[3]

THE RETURN OF JESUS

Many Christians are surprised to learn that Muslims believe in the return of Jesus. There are other similarities between Christian and Muslim eschatology, but there are vast differences, as well. For example, Muslims believe that Jesus will convert the world to Islam when He returns. They also believe that He will kill the Jews and break crosses. They also think that Jesus will declare himself to be a Muslim and then die after forty years.

Even within Islam itself there are great differences with regard to the events that may be associated with the end times. One major point of difference is the return of a figure known as the *Mahdi*; some Muslims believe this figure will return before Jesus does. The Shi'ites, for example, believe that the Mahdi will establish order in the world and turn people toward Islam before Jesus returns. Other Muslims do not believe in the Mahdi at all, and some think he will come when Jesus returns.

The conclusion of human history, according to Muslims, is known as either the final hour or the end times. As is the case with both Judaism and Christianity, Islam foresees a final battle between the nations and the Messiah (both Christianity and Islam regard Jesus as the Messiah, but Judaism does not.

As I pointed out in the preceding chapter, Judaism awaits the coming of the Messiah at the end of days.)

All three faiths share a belief in a future individual who will oppose God and His rule. The name Muslims give to this figure is *Dajjal*; Christians call him the anti-Christ, and Jews use the name of *Armilus*. All three religions believe that the Messiah will defeat this enemy in the last days.

Gog and Magog are presented in the eschatology of all three faiths, as well. (See Ezekiel 38 and 39; Revelation 20; and Surah 18:94, 97; 21:96 in the Koran.) It is believed that Gog and Magog will lead a group of nations against God in the end times. Some Muslims interpret Surah 21:95-98 in the Koran as meaning that Gog and Magog will be composed of Zionist Jews, Trinitarian Christians (viewed as polytheists because of their belief in the Trinity), and all other "infidels" (those who are not Muslims).

THE MAHDI

The Mahdi (aka *Mehdi*) is known as the "guided one." Shi'ites and some Sunnis believe that, alongside Jesus, he will erase all error, injustice, and tyranny from the world. There is some dispute about his role in the end times, however. Sunnis and Shi'ites have found little common ground regarding the Mahdi, who is not mentioned in the Koran at all.

Shia Muslims believe that the Mahdi is the "twelfth Imam"—Muhammad al-Mahdi (aka Muhammad Al-Muntazar—the "hidden imam," who disappeared in AD 878).

The following beliefs regarding the Mahdi are held by many Muslims:

1. He will be a descendant of Muhammad.

2. He will bear the name of Muhammad.

3. His rule will not be long—only seven, nine, eleven, or nineteen years.

Osama bin Laden

4. His coming will be accompanied by the raising of a black standard in Khurasan. (This is described by Kitab al Irshad as follows: "... the Arabs will throw off the reins and take possession of their land, throwing out the foreign authority; the people of Egypt will kill their ruler and destroy Syria; and three standards will dispute over it [Syria]; the standards of Qays and the Arabs will come among the people of Egypt; the standards of Kinda [will go] to Khurasan [modern-day Afghanistan and surrounding regions]; horses will come from the west until they are stabled in al-Hira [a city in Iraq]; the black standards will advance towards them from the east...."[4]

5. When the Mahdi comes, the anti-Christ will appear in the East.

It is reported that Muhammad said this about the Mahdi: "The world will not pass away before the Arabs are ruled by a man [the Mahdi] of my family whose name will be the same as mine."

In a later section we will discuss some of the signs that Muslims believe will precede the arrival of the Mahdi. First, however, let's take a look at one important person that some Muslims believe is the Mahdi.

OSAMA BIN LADEN

According to U.S. military intelligence experts, some Muslims believe that Osama bin Laden is the Mahdi. For example, some of the detainees held at Guantanamo have stated that they believe bin Laden is the "awaited, enlightened one." Some Islamic terrorists have indicated that they are engaging in terrorism because of their belief in the Mahdi and the possibility that he has come to Earth in the form of Osama bin Laden.

It is interesting to note that bin Laden himself has been signing his name as "Osama bin Muhammad bin Laden" since 2001. As I have already pointed out, the Mahdi, according to many Muslims, including Muhammad himself, will bear the name of Muhammad.

Furthermore, it is believed among Muslims that the Mahdi will appear at a time when Islamists are feeling oppressed all over the world. This is such a time, to be sure, and many Muslims believe that the Mahdi's responsibility will be to fight the oppressors, unite Muslims, bring peace and justice to the world, rule over all Arabs, and lead a prayer at Mecca in the presence of Jesus.

The belief that bin Laden is the Mahdi lends credence to the thought that the end times are upon us. It even suggests that the year 2012 could bring about the climax of human history as we know it. (See the epigraph at the beginning of this chapter.)

Dr. Timothy R. Furnish has listed the following characteristics of the Mahdi:

• He will descend from Muhammad through Fatima, Muhammad's daughter.

• He will bear the name of Muhammad.

• He will have a distinct forehead and prominent nose.

• He will be generous and altruistic.

• He will arise in Arabia and will be popularly chosen to lead the Muslims.

• He will withstand an attack by an army from Syria, which will be "swallowed up" by the desert.

• He will fill the Earth with justice and fairness.

• He will reign for five, seven, or nine years, perhaps as a co-ruler with Jesus. After this span of time the last trumpet will sound and the Final Judgment will take place.

It doesn't seem to me that Osama bin Laden fits the above description, except for possibly the distinct forehead and prominent nose. He certainly is not filling the Earth with justice and fairness, and he is not generous and altruistic. He did arise in Arabia, however, and does now bear the name of Muhammad.

SIGNS LEADING TO THE MAHDI'S APPEARANCE ON EARTH

The following are some additional signs that Muslims look for with regard to the Mahdi's advent:

• The red death (the sword) and the white death (the plague) will take place before he comes.

• Several figures will appear on the world stage: the one-eyed Dajjal, the *Sufyani* (a Muslim tyrant from Syria that the Mahdi will have to face). Another figure, *an-Nafs az-Zakiya*—the Pure Soul—will be assassinated.

• The sun will rise in the West, and a star will appear in the East. This star will give out as much light as the moon.

• The Arabs will take possession of their lands and throw out all foreigners.

• A "caller" will call out from Heaven.

• There will be a great conflict that will result in the destruction of Syria.

• Death and fear will afflict people in Baghdad and all of Iraq. A fire will appear in the sky, and redness will cover the Iraqis.

• The heavens will be cleft asunder.

• The planets will be dispersed.

• The seas will pour forth.

• The sepulchers will be overturned.

• The sun will be overthrown.

• The stars will fall.

• The hills will be moved.

Some of the above signs require considerable interpretation, but many have to do with natural disasters on Earth and in the heavens. These are recurring themes in many end-times prophecies.

Some Sunnis believe that the Mahdi will be an ordinary man, who will be born to an ordinary woman. Those who believe in him trust that he will lead a mighty Islamic army against the enemies of Islam.

What is believed about him comes from Islamic tradition and history, not from the Koran. There are many Muslims who believe that he is alive now.

James F. Gauss writes, "The president of Iran, Mahmoud Ahmadinejad, has an apocalyptic mind-set. He has made no secret of his belief that he has a role to play in the End Times and has a maniacal desire to bring about Armageddon and ushering in the return of the Mahdi. He believes he has been called to bring about the cataclysmic destruction of the world, which according to Shi'ite Muslim lore, will result in the return of the 12th Imam or Muslim Messiah or Mahdi. In his invective speech before the United Nations in September 2006, Ahmadinejad's most important words were lost on the non-Muslim world as he invoked the return of the Mahdi:

"'I emphatically declare that today's world, more than ever before, longs for just and righteous people with love for all humanity; and above all longs for the perfect righteous human being and the real savior who has been promised to all peoples and who will establish justice, peace and brotherhood on the planet. Oh, Almighty God, all men and women are your creatures and you have ordained their guidance and salvation. Bestow upon humanity that thirsts for justice, the perfect human being promised to all by you, and make us among his followers and among those who strive for his return and his cause'"[5] (From *Islam & Christianity—a Revealing Contrast* by James F. Gauss, Ph.D.)

I highly recommend that you read Dr. Gauss's book, which provides the reader with a comprehensive overview of the differences between Christianity and Islam, and reveals many things about Islamic influences in our world today.

This "perfect human being" to whom the President of Iran refers is, in all likelihood, none other than the Mahdi. Dr. Gauss goes on to say, "The purpose of the Mahdi is not to bring salvation to the lost but, rather, to usher in an age of world destruction so that only Muslims will inherit the earth. 'Ahmadinejad,' according to WorldNetDaily, 'is on record as stating he believes he is to have a personal role in ushering in the age of the Mahdi. In a November 16, 2005, speech in Tehran, he said he sees his main mission in life as to 'pave the path for the glorious reappearance of Imam Mahdi, may Allah hasten his appearance.'"[6]

Ahmadinejad's personal mission is, therefore, aimed at the destruction of our present world, the annihilation of Christians and Jews, and the rule and reign of Islam everywhere. His pursuit of nuclear technology could well be an integral part of this plan.

THE EMERGENCE OF THE SUFYANI

One other important figure in end-times events is predicted to arise when Jesus and the Mahdi come to Earth. This figure is the Sufyani, a descendant of Abu Sufyan. According to the prophecy, he will be from Damascus, Syria.

The Sufyani will be a tyrant, who will kill children and rip out the bellies of women. It is said that when he hears about the Mahdi, he will send an army to seize and kill him. However, the desert will "swallow" him and his army before he is able to reach the Mahdi.

Abu Hurairah (aka Hurayrah) has given the following prophecy [from Muhammad] regarding the Sufyani: "A man will emerge from the depths of Damascus. He will be called Sufyani. Most of those who follow him will be from the tribe of Kalb. He will kill by ripping the stomachs of women and even kill the children. A man from my family will appear in the Haram, the news of his advent will reach the Sufyani and he will send to him one of his armies. He [referring to Imam Mahdi] will defeat them. They will then travel with whoever remains until they come to a desert and they will be swallowed.

None will be saved except the one who had informed the others about them."[7]

WHEN WILL THE END COME?

Though there are no precise dates given in Islamic literature with regard to the end times, there is a sense that the end is near, particularly when one considers the potential roles of men like Osama bin Laden and Mahmoud Ahmadinejad on today's world stage. The Koran has this to say: "Lo! The Hour is surely coming. But I [Allah] will to keep it hidden, that every soul may be rewarded for that which it striveth [to achieve]" (Surah 20:15).

Recent events in Pakistan, with the Taliban moving even closer to Pakistan's site of nuclear weapons, have sounded an alarm signal around the world.

The Koran also says, "Men ask of you the Hour. Say: The knowledge of it is with Allah only. What can convey [the knowledge] unto thee? It may be that the Hour is nigh" (Surah 30:63).

These passages are comparable to the words of Jesus, who said, *"But of that day and hour knoweth no man, no, not the angels of heaven, but my Father only"* (Matthew 24:36, KJV).

AN ISLAMIC VIEW OF JESUS

According to some Islamic teaching, in the end of time Jesus and the armies of Mahdi will conquer the world and force all those who remain to become Muslims. The Dajjal— an anti-Christ figure—and his force of seventy thousand Jews will be destroyed, according to some Islamic teachings.

They also believe that Jesus will kill "the pigs" (the infidels), break crosses, and kill Jews. They go on to say that Jesus will get married, live forty years, and have children. When He dies, according to these teachings, He will be buried next to Muhammad in Medina.[8]

JESUS THE CHRIST

Even though many Muslims believe that Jesus will play a prominent role in end-time events, it is important to realize that they do not view Him as the Savior. In fact, Muslims disregard the concept of a personal Savior altogether. Sin, to them, is a personal issue; according to Islam, each individual possesses the ability to change with God's help. It is the good works that are listed in the Koran that serve to purify the inner being.

Jesus is seen simply as a prophet, even though they do call Him "the Messiah." Muslims do not believe that Jesus died on the cross. Instead, they think that someone else died on the cross, and Allah took Jesus directly to Heaven, where He was to remain until the end times. The name they give to Jesus is *Isa*.

Isa is mentioned several times in the Koran, but Muslims firmly deny that He is the Son of God.

JIHAD—A "HOLY WAR"

A *jihad* is a holy war. This term may refer to an inner struggle or a full-scale conflict between individuals and/or nations. In the latter case, a jihad involves killing in defense of Islam.

Often, the word jihad is used when a Muslim is focused on getting rid of an infidel or infidels. Such a killing is viewed by many Muslims as being a meritorious act that will take the Jihadist to paradise and many eternal rewards. Ultimately, the goal of a jihad is to lead people to Islam.

A correspondent for the *Baltimore Sun*, James E. Goodby, wrote, "It's only a matter of time…. That's what the experts say when asked whether a terrorist organization might detonate an atom bomb in an American city."[9]

It's only a matter of time!

An ardent fundamentalist Muslim is likely to consider such an act to be an honorable form of jihad, as the terrorists who flew airplanes into the towers of the World Trade Center did on September 11, 2001. Graham Allison wrote in his book, *Nuclear Terrorism*, "If policy makers in Washington keep doing what they are currently doing about the [nuclear] threat, a nuclear terrorist attack on America is likely to occur in the next decade. And if one lengthens the time frame, a nuclear strike is inevitable…. We do not have the luxury of hoping the problem will go away."[10]

There is no doubt that such a nuclear attack would bring America to its knees, and it could well usher in the end of the age. Could this scenario develop in 2012?

"We get to think of life as an inexhaustible well. Yet everything happens only a certain number of times, and a very

small number, really. How many more times will you remember a certain afternoon of your childhood, some afternoon that's so deeply a part of your being that you can't even conceive of your life without it? Perhaps four or five times more, perhaps not even that. How many more times will you watch the full moon rise? Perhaps twenty. And yet it all seems limitless" (Paul Bowles).

"It's like things are in the world. Hopes fail. An end comes. We have only a little time to wait now" (J.R.R. Tolkien).

Endnotes

1. http://www.diagnosis2012.co.uk/new3htm
2. *What Does Islam Believe About the End?* http://www.truthnet. org/islam/Islam-Bible/4Islam beliefs/index.htm
3. http://2012-predictions-review.blogspot.com/2008/05/ muslims-and-islam
4. *The Infallibles.* http://www.al-islam.org/masoom/bios/ 12thimam.html
5. Gauss, James F. *Islam & Christianity—a Revealing Contrast.* Bridge-Logos Publishers, Alachua, Florida, 2009.
6. Ibid.
7. *Imam Mahdi and the Signs That Will Precede Him.* http:// www.inter-islam.org/faith/mahdil.htm
8. *What Does Islam Believe About the End?* http://www. truthnet.org/islam/Islam-Bible/4Islambeliefs/index.htm
9. Gauss, James F. *Islam & Christianity –a Revealing Contrast.* Bridge-Logos Publishers, Alachua, Florida, 2009.
10. Ibid.

Other Resources That Were Consulted in the Preparation of This Chapter

1. *In the Name of God, Most Gracious, Most Merciful.* http://www.submission.org/suras/app25.html

2. *2012 Predictions Review.* http://2012-predictions-review.blogspot.com/2008/05/muslims-and-islam.html

3. *Sufiyani.* http://en.wikipedia.org/wiki/Sufyani

4. *Is bin Laden the 'Mahdi'?* http://www.worldnetdaily.com/news/article.asp?ARTICLE_ID=34469

5. *Islam and the End Times.* http://www.theendtimesproject.com/islamandtheendti.html

6. *Islam Is Key to Unlocking the Secrets of Ancient End Time Prophecies.* http:www.theopenpress.com/index.php?a=press&id=23228

7. *Mahdi.* http://en.wikipedia.org/wiki/Mahdi

8. *End Time.* http://en.wikipedia.org/wiki/End_times

Additional Resources You May Wish to Consult

1. *History of Islamic Philosophy* by Henry Corbin. (Translated by Liadain Sherrard and Philip Sherrartd. Kegan Paul International, 1993.

2. *The Life of Imam Al-Mahdi* by al-Qarashi, Baqir Sharif. (Translated by Syed Athar Husain S.H. Risvi. Ansariyan Publications, 2006.

3. *Holiest Wars: Islamic Mahdis, Jihad and Osama bin Laden* by Timothy Furnish. (Westport: Praeger, 2005.

13

THE WEB BOT PROJECT

*The Web Bot Project is probably the only scientific method
we have of predicting the future and has had some
surprisingly accurate past predictions.*
FROM HTTP://WWW.ABOVETOPSECRET.COM/FORUM[1]

WHAT IS THE WEB BOT PROJECT?

Not long ago while I was having my hair cut, the stylist
said, "I think we are in for a major disaster of some sort." Her
statement reflects what numbers of people are thinking today.
These feelings are discerned and reflected in the findings of the
Web Bot Project, as you will see within this chapter.

The Web Bot Project was started in the late 1990's. Though
it was originally designed to track trends within the stock
market, it has expanded to cover predictions regarding natural
disasters, societal trends, and changes all over the world. It uses
a system that involves Internet "spiders," agents, "robots,"
and wanderers, which "crawl" all over the Internet to see what
kind of chatter is taking place and to uncover trends that point
to the future.

The name "web bot" comes from the last word in World
Wide Web joined with the second syllable in the word
"robot." The bot (or robot) performs simple tasks that are
highly repetitive, as it searches for key words and phrases.
This is known as web spidering; through this means the bot

can gather, analyze, and file pieces of information from the Internet much faster than human beings can.

Like a search engine, the bot-spider searches for particular kinds of words. By looking at patterns of behavior, hot topics in chat rooms, discussion groups, translation sites, and the like, these "spiders" endeavor to foretell events before they happen. In some ways, this is like the Elliott Time Wave I discussed in an earlier chapter in that it endeavors to tap into the collective unconscious of people everywhere by looking for certain target words and their synonyms and seeing what trends are emerging in society.

The Web Bot Project gathers these words, transfers them into numbers, and develops a series of "scatter charts." Over an extended period of time, these scatter charts begin to join together into highly concentrated areas. Each dot on the scatter chart might represent one word or several hundred words. Eventually, the researcher is able to come up with a series of phrases related to the word(s) and thereby provide predictions for the future.

These predictions are based on data gathered from people all over the world. Therefore, the Web Bot Project simply identifies what people are thinking about a given topic, and it then reflects those feelings in the form of predictions. Some of these predictions are vague, while others are specific.

There's a sense in which this process could be considered to be very much like a self-fulfilling prophecy. It is, therefore, an anticipatory kind of foretelling that is based on what people are expecting. However, there are times when the Web Bot Project is able to determine what people are actually planning to do by analyzing "chatter" it discovers on the Web. For example, prior to a terrorist attack, the Web Bot might be able to make fairly precise predictions about terrorism based on what it "hears" via Internet chat rooms and the like.

In the paragraphs that follow, I recount some of the accurate predictions that have been made by the Web Bot Project.

In June 2001, the Project said that a catastrophic event would occur within the next sixty-ninety days. On September 11, 2001, the Twin Towers of the World Trade Center fell.

In 2003, the Web Bot Project said that a major maritime disaster would occur. Soon thereafter the Space Shuttle *Columbia* disaster took place (February 1, 2003).

It also predicted the 2003 blackout in New York City.

Prior to the anthrax scare, the Project predicted that there would be an attack on the U.S. Congress.

In 2004, the Web Bot Project stated that there would be an earthquake that would be followed by a rising of water. This was just before the devastating tsunami, which took place in December 2004.

It predicted Hurricane Katrina in 2005.

There was even a Web Bot prediction that said that Vice President Cheney would be involved with a gunshot wounding. Many thought that this meant that someone would attempt to assassinate him, but the truth of the matter was that the vice president fired the shot—a shot that wounded his friend.

One of the most recent accurate predictions given by the Web Bot Project declared that there would be a global economic collapse that would begin in the autumn of 2008. This did, indeed, take place, and the entire world reacted to the decline of the U.S. dollar. (For more on this subject, please read *The Day the Dollar Dies* by Willard Cantelon, published by Bridge-Logos in Alachua, Florida.)

The Web Bot Project went on to predict that there would be a global replay of the Great Depression. We have certainly come close to the fulfillment of this prediction.

In relationship to this dire economic forecast, the Project predicted that Americans would be impacted by great stress, bordering on post-traumatic stress disorder. It is true that everyone was stunned by the dramatic changes in the world economy that began to be revealed in 2008.

The Web Bot Project also predicted that the mood of the populace would improve after the presidential election of 2008. Indeed, there was much elation and jubilation in the United States and around the world over the election of President Barack Obama.

The Year of Transformation—2009

A disclaimer that appears on a website that does Web Bot predictions states, "We don't make the future—we just try to see it coming."[2] The same site refers to AD 2009 as the "Year of Transformation." This term suggests that the life situations of many people will be radically different by the end of the year.

What are some of the specifics that might be involved in this transformation? Here is what the Web Bot has to say:

• U.S. economic collapse is possible due to the collapse of the housing bubble, the debt-instrument-bubble collapse, and the value of the dollar. (A specific prediction is that as a result of falling revenues, there will be 30-40 percent decreases in government size and services.)

• An unspecified global coastal event is predicted to occur during 2009.

• Various governmental secrets will be revealed from NASA and other high-government offices. (It is predicted that "whistle blowers" will have a role in this.)

• A return to a simple lifestyle will become commonplace.

• It will be a global "summer of hell." Some regions will be without power and food. There will be numerous "summer shakes"—earthquakes.

• Government services will falter as the summer winds down.

• Many government workers will walk off the job.

• Social Security and other government payments may decline or temporarily stop in the autumn of 2009.

- Cooperative living will emerge in many small communities during September.
- Internet availability will become sporadic in October.[3]

A WORLDWIDE CALAMITY WILL TAKE PLACE IN 2012!

Let's take a look to see what the Web Bot Project has to say about AD 2012. Based on pointers that were uncovered by the Web Bot related to the Apocalypse that is predicted by many individuals and groups, the Project states that a worldwide calamity is likely to take place sometime during 2012.

To be more specific, the Web Bot Project has predicted that a planetary line-up will occur in 2012, and this will cause extraordinary solar events that will include an output of enormous energy, gamma-ray bursts, and dangerous plasma discharges. These things, if true, could well bring dire times upon our planet.

Some of these predictions are based on scientific evidence, such as the fact that the sun and the Earth will be in direct alignment with a black hole in the center of our galaxy during 2012. This could result in the magnetic shifts we discussed in an earlier chapter, which might possibly bring about a polar reversal. Also, the prediction about the coming Solar Maximus figures into this.

Many of the predictions that have come forth from the Web Bot Project relate to global finance, and we are already seeing many of these "prophecies" coming true. The recent multi-billion-dollar governmental bailouts of financial institutions and other corporations have put the U.S. economy in a very precarious position. Will this continue to destabilize our future and put the lives of many people around the world in jeopardy? Has this already begun?

According to the Web Bot Project, things may well go from bad to worse.

Can the Web Bot make accurate predictions? The truth is that it already has. However, it is important to realize that its predictions are not supernatural at all; they simply reflect the feelings and attitudes of people.

The Web Bot Project has many useful applications, to be sure, but we must remember that it is limited with regard to what it can reveal about the future. Nonetheless, it is able to pick up on trends and make predictions based on these.

"Tomorrow belongs to the people who prepare for it today" (African proverb).

"Who knows but the world may end tonight" (Robert Browning).

Endnotes

1. http://www.abovetopsecret.com/forum
2. www.halfpasthuman.com/www.urgansurvival.com
3. Ibid.

Other Resources That Were Consulted in the Preparation of This Chapter

1. http://en.wikipedia.org/wiki/Internet_bot
2. *Is the Web Bot Project a Tool for Future Predictions?* http://www.islandcrisis.net/2009/02/web-bot-project-tool-future-predictions-2009
3. *Web Bot Predictions for 2009.* http:www.realufos.net/2008/07/web-bot-predictions-for-2009-year-of.html
4. *Web Bot—What Is It? Can It Predict Stuff?* http:www.dailycommonsense.com/web-bot-what-is-it-can-it-predict-stuff.
5. *Dark Government.* http://www.darkgovernment.com/news/web-bot-project-predicting-huge-natural-disaster-for-December.

14

THE BIBLE AND PROPHECY

*No one knows about that day or hour, not even the angels
in heaven, nor the Son, but only the Father. Be on guard! Be
alert! You do not know when that day will come.... I say to
you, I say to everyone: "Watch!"*
JESUS, FROM MARK 13:32-37, NIV

COMMON PROPHETIC THEMES

The first thirteen chapters of this book present end-time prophecies from a variety of sources, such as religious groups, ancient cultures, individuals, science, and the Internet. As you have no doubt noticed, several recurring themes are found in these various prophecies. Do these similarities give confirmation to these predictions? From what source(s) have they been derived?

There are other prophets and prophecies we have not looked at, and we will give brief mention to only a couple of them here. For example, Edgar Cayce, who gave more than fourteen thousand readings in his lifetime, predicted major Earth changes and unusual weather patterns from 1958 to 1998. He believed he saw, in the aftermath of these phenomena, violent storms and earthquakes occurring more frequently than ever before. He believed these changes would be precursors to a coming pole shift.

Another end-times prophecy comes from the Masonic Lodge, which teaches that the two final witnesses that are mentioned in the Book of Revelation (see Revelation 11:3) will appear during 2009. These two married witnesses will be persecuted by the world religious community. According to the Masons, they will eventually be killed by "beast power" sometime in 2012. These prophecies of the Freemasons also predict major Earth changes, and they tell us that the two witnesses will be approximately sixty-six years old at the time of their deaths.[1]

Jesus' epigraph at the beginning of this chapter tells us that only one Person (the heavenly Father) knows the day and the hour when things on this Earth will come to a conclusion. Jesus does not know, and neither do the angels. However, Jesus provided us with a list of signs that will help us to know when the end times are approaching. He also told us to watch for those signs, so we will know what to anticipate. In light of these admonitions, it is good that we are looking for end-time answers in this book.

This chapter takes a close look at what Jesus, the Bible, and Bible scholars have to say about eschatology. It focuses mainly on writings that are found within the New Testament.

Some of the prophets we've studied point to a cataclysmic time at the end of history when the world could end or an entirely new age will begin. This predicted cataclysm might be caused by natural disasters, such as earthquakes, floods, volcanoes, tsunamis, wind storms, meteors, and the like, or it might be initiated by human beings using nuclear or biological weapons.

The Bible, as we noted in the chapter regarding Hebrew prophecies, seems to concur with many of these predictions. What are we to believe about the end times? What does the holy Bible have to say?

Not knowing the day or the hour flies in the face of those who seem quite certain that the end of time will occur on December 21, 2012. It is important to remember, however, that only God the Father knows when that time will come.

BIBLE CODE PROPHECIES

In an effort to know what the future holds some researchers who are known as cryptographers have looked into the Bible for certain sequences and patterns that they believe will lead to accurate predictions about the future. These analysts have determined that the Bible contains coded information about the future.

Bible codes are also known as Torah codes. They consist of words, phrases, and clusters of words and phrases that are perceived to be written in coded form within the Bible.

The decoding process involves a method that is known as the Equidistant Letter Sequence (ELS), which consists of selecting letters from the text at equal spacing from each other and using a skip number. Spaces and punctuation are ignored, and then a word that is based on these units is spelled out.

Sir Isaac Newton was one of the first seekers of hidden biblical messages. He said that the Bible is, "… a cryptogram set by the Almighty—a riddle of the Godhead of past and future events divinely foreordained. This prophecy is called the Revelation, with respect to the Scripture of Truth, which Daniel was commanded to shut up and seal, till the end of time. Until that time comes, the Lamb is opening the seals."

The thirteenth-century Spanish rabbi Bachya ben Asher discovered the first ELS in the Bible. Many other rabbis continued to develop this system through the centuries. One mathematician, Eliyahu Rips of the Hebrew University of Jerusalem, went into great depth, along with a few others, in his research into the presumed Bible Code.[2]

Several books have been published about this topic. One of these, *The Bible Code*, was written by Michael Drosnin. It was published in 1997. It's sequel, *The Bible Code II*, was published in 2002.

By examining the Bible Code, Drosnin accurately predicted the assassination of Israel's Prime Minister Yitzhak Rabin in 1995. He also made other predictions that did not come true.[3]

Certain interpretations of the Bible Code have led to predictions about AD 2012. Some of these are:

• The Earth will be annihilated by a large comet that will hit Canada.

• The axis of the Earth will tilt and tip.

• Seismic activity will tear the Earth to pieces.

Lawrence E. Joseph writes, "The Bible tells us that God will annihilate the Earth in 2012." He bases this statement on Drosnin's conclusions, as cited above.[4]

According to one researcher, the Bible Code gives specific predictions about the times in which we are currently living. Please bear in mind, however, that I am not a cryptanalyst, and those who are cryptographers vary a great deal with regard to their interpretations of Bible codes.

That being said, let's see what some cryptographers believe about our present era. These researchers tell us that the Bible strongly suggests that AD 2007, 2008, and 2009 are years of extreme weather patterns and major economic problems. (These predictions have certainly come true.)

These same cryptographers feel certain that the Book of Isaiah predicts the nuclear destruction of Jerusalem in AD 2010. They also say that Israel will launch a massive counterattack.

Some natural disasters are predicted to take place within that same year:

• An asteroid impact.

• A great earthquake in Yellowstone National Park.

• The destruction of America.

• It will be a year filled with gloom, terror, and darkness.

• A massive loss of life will occur, and there is a good possibility of a pole shift.

One interpreter of the Bible Code has indicated that four billion people (the majority of people on Earth) will die by

2012. These deaths, according to one interpretation, will be caused by an asteroid or a comet hitting the Earth. Now let's take a look at some of the things Jesus said about the last days.

THE PROPHECIES OF JESUS

The disciples asked Jesus a question that many are asking today, *"Tell us when will this happen, and what will be the sign of your coming and of the end of the age"* (Matthew 24:3, NIV).

This is a question that people have asked through the ages, and certainly many people are asking it today, as well. What was Jesus' answer? He said, *"Watch out that no one deceives you. For many will come in my name, claiming, 'I am the Christ,' and will deceive many"* (Matthew 24:5, NIV). (See also Matthew 24:11.)

Is this happening today? We can give an emphatic affirmative answer to this question by citing numerous people who were and are in the "false Christ" category. Certainly the pastor of People's Temple, Jim Jones, was one, and so are many New Age teachers. Some Jewish rabbis have claimed to be the Messiah, as well.

Jesus said, *"You will hear of wars and rumors of wars, but see to it that you are not alarmed. Such things must happen, but the end is still to come. Nation will rise against nation, and kingdom against kingdom"* (Matthew 24:6-7, NIV).

This is a clear prediction that gives a preview of events that have recently transpired and are transpiring in our world today. The pockmarks of war filled the Earth during the twentieth century. Two world wars, the Korean Conflict, and the Vietnam War were only some of the conflicts that took place during that century, and untold millions were slaughtered all over the globe. More people were killed through warfare during the twentieth century than have been killed in any other century.

Militarism continues today in the Middle East, Africa, South America, and many other places. We are living in a time of wars and rumors of war, and terrorism is on the upswing in so many places. Violence and bloodshed fill the newspapers on a daily basis. Drug wars have taken the lives of many in Mexico and throughout Latin America.

Jesus said, *"There will be famines and earthquakes in various places"* (Matthew 24:7, NIV). Look at the continent of Africa, where people are starving to death in huge numbers on a daily basis. Many people all over the world lack food and other basic necessities of life.

Earthquakes are becoming very frequent, and many scientists believe that several regions of the globe will be impacted by huge earthquakes in the very near future. While I was writing this book, for example, a major earthquake in L'Aquila, Italy, killed nearly three hundred people and devastated this quaint medieval village.

Earthquakes are occurring with greater intensity and frequency, and Earth tremors occur somewhere almost every day.

Jesus said, *"All these are the beginnings of birth pains. Then you will be handed over to be persecuted and put to death, and you will be hated by all nations because of me. At that time many will turn away from the faith and will betray and hate each other, and many false prophets will appear and deceive many people. Because of the increase of wickedness, the love of most will grow cold, but he who stands firm to the end will be saved."* (Matthew 24:8-13, NIV)

More martyrdoms of Christians are taking place around the world now than ever before, particularly in Muslim areas. Some Christians are being persecuted severely and many are going through times of great testing and tribulation. The pain and hatred that Christians will have to endure will become increasingly intense as the end of days draws near.

We are seeing a decline in interest in Christianity in the present time as well as a rise in false teachings and deception. Wickedness is increasing, and it seems as if new forms of evil are emerging on an almost-daily basis. These things are happening to believers as well as unbelievers. Mass murders and serial killings seem to be happening more often, many times for no apparent reason, and it seems that few people can be trusted. One young father said to me, "I even worry about taking my daughters to church. Who can you trust anymore?"

Here are some recent statistics that reveal certain downward societal trends related to morality that are taking place in our times. These figures are based upon an average week in the life of Americans:[5]

- 28% used profanity in public
- 20% gambled
- 19% viewed "adult" or pornographic images
- 12% gossiped
- 12% got drunk
- 11% lied
- 9% had sex with someone who is not their spouse
- 8% retaliated for something someone said or did

David Kinnaman writes, "We face stiff challenges. Our nation has perfected a moral system that is based on convenience, feelings, and selfishness. The consistent deterioration of the Bible as the source of moral truth has led to a nation where people have become independent judges of right and wrong. It is not likely that America will return to a more traditional moral code until the nation experiences significant pain from its poor moral choices."[6]

The nation and the world are experiencing that pain now. Are these the birth pains that Jesus refers to?

Every day we read of horrendous killings taking place. Abortion has become commonplace. In an attempt to kill the sense of hopelessness that many are experiencing, thousands opt to end their lives through suicide. Today's news reports that a female Sunday school teacher may have molested and killed an eight-year-old girl who was in her Sunday school class. The woman is the granddaughter of that church's pastor.

Men and women are killing their children, and random acts of violence in schools, malls, restaurants, along the highways, and even in churches make everyone wonder if we are safe anywhere. Suicide bombings in the Middle East and elsewhere are leading to great fear and panic.

Why is all this happening today? Are there any solutions to these problems?

Jesus said, *"And this gospel of the kingdom will be preached in the whole world as a testimony to all nations, and then the end will come"* (Matthew 24:14, NIV). Satellite television and the Internet are enabling the Gospel of Jesus Christ to be preached literally around the world.

Radio broadcasts beam the gospel message to some of the most remote places on Earth, and missionaries are gathering a harvest in all the nations. Clearly, the fulfillment of this prophecy has become more likely in our present age than ever before.

Let me recommend another book to you here. It is written by Peter Tsukahira, and it deals with Israel and end-times revival. It is published by Bridge-Logos and is entitled *God's Tsunami.*[7]

The prophecies of Jesus that we've just reviewed are from Matthew 24, which goes on to describe other signs of the end times. Jesus said, *"For then there will be great distress, unequaled from the beginning of the world until now—and never to be equaled again. If those days had not been cut short, no one would survive, but for the sake of the elect those days will be shortened"* (Matthew 24:21-22, NIV).

It is clear from this passage that the end of all things will be an act of God's mercy—a blessing for those who believe in the Son of God. It will be their deliverance from the worst circumstances imaginable.

Jesus had a great deal to say about the end times. Obviously, He wanted us to be prepared for what is to come. Let's take a brief look at some of His other prophecies.

Jesus wants us to be vigilant, to be aware of the signs of the times. He said to the Pharisees and Sadducees, *"When evening comes, you say, 'It will be fair weather, for the sky is red,' and in the morning, 'Today it will be stormy, for the sky is red and overcast.' You know how to interpret the appearance of the sky, but you cannot interpret the signs of the times"* (Matthew 16:2-3, NIV).

In Mark 13, while teaching about the end times, Jesus warned us to watch out, to be on our guard, to be alert, and to be vigilant. He wants His people to prepare themselves and to be ready for the end.

Jesus said, *"You also must be ready, because the Son of Man will come at an hour when you do not expect him"* (Luke 12:40, NIV). Are you ready? How can you best prepare for His coming?

Here is a definite warning from the Son of God: *"Just as it was in the days of Noah, so also will it be in the days of the Son of Man. People were eating, drinking, marrying and being given in marriage up to the day Noah entered the ark. Then the flood came and destroyed them all. It was the same in the days of Lot. People were eating and drinking, buying and selling, planting and building. But the day Lot left Sodom, fire and sulfur rained down from heaven and destroyed them all. It will be just like this on the day the Son of Man is revealed."* (Luke 17:26-30, NIV)

Luke 21 is filled with the prophecies of Jesus about the end times in which He warns His disciples to avoid deception and not to be fearful when talk about wars and revolutions takes place. He mentions earthquakes, famines, and pestilences that will occur, and describes startling events in the heavens that will transpire. (As I write this, a possible pandemic of Swine Flu has begun—a dreadful pestilence, indeed.) He said that persecution will come to believers, but advises us not to worry about how to defend ourselves. He points out that Christians will be betrayed by those who are closest to us, and, as a result of this, some will be put to death. He declared that believers will be greatly hated.

Then He gave a particular sign that we should be looking for: *"When you see Jerusalem being surrounded by armies, you will know that its desolation is near"* (Luke 21:20, NIV). He goes on to say, *"Men will faint from terror, apprehensive of what is coming on the world, for the heavenly bodies will be shaken. At that time they will see the Son of Man coming in a cloud with power and great glory. When these things begin to take place, stand up and lift up your heads, because your redemption is drawing near."* (Luke 21:26-28, NIV)

In effect, Jesus has given us "the end of the story" without telling us exactly when it will take place. However, He has told us about various evidences we should be looking for. The apostles of the New Testament have also tried to prepare us for the last days. In the next sections of this book we will take a look at some of their writings.

THE END OF ALL THINGS IS AT HAND

A friend of mine, Dr. Richard Booker, has written a fascinating book entitled, *The End of All Things Is at Hand— Are You Ready?* I recommend that you read this book for more information about the end times and for help in getting prepared for that event.[8]

Richard writes, "As we look at the conditions of our world, many believe that we are living in the end times. The Lord burdened my heart to write about these end-time events with a holy awe of His presence, His plans, and His purposes for the future. Because the God of Abraham, the God of Isaac, and the God of Jacob is outside of time, He knows the end of time from the beginning of time (Isaiah 46:9-10). He has written prophetic events in the Bible to awaken us, alert us, and inform us about the future."

The title for his book comes from this Scripture: *"But the end of all things is at hand; be ye therefore sober, and watch unto prayer"* (1 Peter 4:7, KJV).

Dr. Booker lists ten key prophetic signs that he has found in the both the Old and New Testaments:

• The return of Jews to their homeland.
• The repossession of Jerusalem by the Jews.
• The rebuilding of the Temple in Jerusalem.
• The establishment of a one-world government.
• The recognition of a one-world religion.
• The northern invasion of Israel.
• An increase in worldwide travel and knowledge.
• The rise of false prophets and an increase in occult activity.
• The Church will become apostate.
• The moral breakdown of society.

These are just some of the prophetic signs that we can use to discern when we are in the end times. How many of these signs do we see today?

Since the nation of Israel was founded in 1948, many Jews have returned to their homeland. In the last three decades of the twentieth century, there was a mass exodus of Russian Jews (approximately one million), who sought refuge in Israel. This is continuing today in fulfillment of the prophecy that was given by Jeremiah: *"'So then, the days are coming,' declares the Lord, 'when people will no longer say, 'As surely as the Lord lives, who brought the Israelites up out of Egypt,' but they will say, 'As surely as the Lord lives, who brought the descendants of Israel up out of the land of the north [Russia] and out of all the countries where he had banished them.' Then they will live in their own land."* (Jeremiah 23:7-8, NIV)

The Jews truly repossessed Jerusalem after the Six-day War of 1967. It was the first time the Holy City came under Jewish control in almost two thousand years. (See Luke 21:24.)

Many groups are already working toward the fulfillment of the prophecy about the rebuilding of the Temple. The blueprints have been drawn and temple garments have been woven. Plans are underway for the laying of the cornerstone. (See Isaiah 2:2-3.)

The United Nations, the World Trade Organization, the World Court, the European Union, and many other international agencies could well be precursors to the full-scale development of a one-world government. (See Daniel 7.)

The prophecy about a one-world religion could be fulfilled in a variety of ways, and one wonders if this has already begun, because the emphasis on New Age spirituality is increasing, as is the spread of Islam around the globe. When times get tough, people are apt to turn to anything for support. This could well involve following a religious leader, who promises great things to them. (See Revelation 13 and 17.)

The invasion of Israel could certainly happen at any time from so many different directions. However, many Christian scholars believe that the invasion will come from the north, and it will involve a federation of nations that is led by Russia. (See Ezekiel 38 and 39.)

Worldwide travel and knowledge are accelerating very rapidly. The Lord told the Prophet Daniel to *"... close up and seal the words of the scroll until the time of the end. Many will go here and there to increase knowledge"* (Daniel 12:4, NIV).

Billy Graham said, "Ninety percent of all the engineers and scientists who have ever lived are alive today." Whether this statistic holds true in our present age or not, the evangelist was pointing to the increase of knowledge and information that is clearly taking place today.

As a publisher, I am well aware of the proliferation of knowledge through books and the Internet. Thousands of new books are produced around the world each month. In fact, 172,000 new books are published in theh U.S. each year.

False prophets, cults, and the occult are recruiting and deceiving people all over the world. It is amazing to see how so many people, even the well educated, can be so easily deceived. Take, for example, the suicidal cult known as Heaven's Gate, whose members committed suicide in the hope that they would be able to ride away via the Hale-Bopp comet. (See Matthew 24.)

The umbrella of Christianity covers many different sects and denominations. Paul wrote, *"Concerning the coming of our Lord Jesus Christ and our being gathered to him, we ask you, brothers, not to become easily unsettled or alarmed by some prophecy, report or letter supposed to have come from us, saying that the day of the Lord has already come. Don't let anyone deceive you in any way, for that day will not come, until the rebellion occurs and the man of lawlessness is revealed, the man doomed to destruction. He will oppose and exalt himself over everything that is called God or is worshiped, so that he sets himself up in God's temple, proclaiming himself to be God."* (2 Thessalonians 2:1-4, NIV)

This "rebellion" refers to an apostate church, which is developing in our time. Apostasy takes place when those who call themselves Christians begin to abandon the biblical foundations of their creed. This is happening in so many denominations today, and some churches even advocate certain sins and blasphemies.

The "man of lawlessness" in this passage is the anti-Christ—the Beast of the Book of Revelation. Starting out as a man of peace, he will ultimately cause great turmoil on the Earth until his final destruction, which is described in Revelation 20:10.

We have already mentioned the breakdown of morality, which is taking place in society and even in the Church. There are pastors, for example, who deny the central tenets of

Christianity and teach their members to do the same. Some do not even believe that Jesus is the Messiah. Homosexuality is embraced as an acceptable lifestyle, and at least one Episcopal bishop has proudly proclaimed that he is gay. The New Age Movement has found its way into mainstream Christianity, as well. (See 2 Timothy 3:1-5.)

The prophetic signs we've just examined are key pointers to the end times. There are others, as well, which I will briefly mention here:

• A two-hundred-million-man army will arise in the East. (See Revelation 9:16.) It is believed by many that this refers to the Chinese army, which numbers in the millions.

• The redevelopment of the Roman Empire. The European Union could well be the fulfillment of this prophecy. (See Daniel 2.)

• The return of the Hebrew language to Israel. While Hebrew was once considered to be a "dead language," it is now being taught and spoken throughout Israel. (See Zephaniah 3:9.)

• The reappearance of "the red heifer." The Book of Numbers tells us that a red heifer is required to be used in the process of purification. It is said that the first red heifer in two thousand years was born in May 1997, and another one was born in Israel in March 2002. (See Numbers 19:2-7.)

• The return of Ethiopian Jews to Israel. Operation Moses in 1984 saw the airlift of fifteen thousand Jews, who had fled to refugee camps in the Sudan. This was followed by Operation Solomon in 1991, which was responsible for flying twenty thousand Jews to Israel from Ethiopia. Another airlift in June 1999 transported the three thousand remaining members of the Quara Jewish community from Ethiopia to Israel. (See Zephaniah 3:10-11.)

• The rise of Russia. Though Russia has had some recent setbacks, it appears to be on the rise again in our present age. According to biblical prophecy, the Russian nation will become very prominent in the end times. It will be a strong nation with a strong army. (See Ezekiel 38:2-8.)

• The mark of the Beast. New technologies lead me to think that this prophecy is in the process of being fulfilled: *"He [the Beast] also forced everyone, small and great, rich and poor, free and slave, to receive a mark on his right hand or on his forehead, so that no one could buy or sell unless he had the mark, which is the name of the beast or the number of his name"* (Revelation 13:16-17, NIV). Some people have recently received a biochip implant in their skin, which contains a small radio transmitter that transmits a personal ID number to a receiver. It would appear that people are becoming increasingly open to the idea of having such an implant that might well be perceived to be a vehicle for greater security and for providing medical information in the event of an emergency. The technology for the fulfillment of this process is in place. How it will be applied remains to be seen, however.

How have these prophetic signs affected your view of the end times? Are you troubled by what you have read? If so, you will want to read the next chapter, which will help you to see that there is no need to fear or to be anxious about the future. There are steps you can take to prepare for what is to come.

"People are afraid of the future, of the unknown. If a man faces up to it, and takes the dare of the future, he can have some control over his destiny. That's an exciting idea to me, better than waiting with everyone else to see what's going to happen" (John H. Glenn).

Endnotes

1. *What's New?* http://www.diagnosis2012.co.uk/new3.htm
2. Joseph, Lawrence E. *The Mystery of 2012,* "The Bible Code." Sounds True, Inc. Boulder, Colorado, 2007.
3. Ibid.
4. Ibid.
5. Kinnaman, David. "Morality in America—for Better and Worse." *Rev,* May-June, 2009.
6. Ibid.
7. Tsukahira, Peter. *God's Tsunami.* Bridge-Logos Publishers, Alachua, Florida, 2009.
8. Booker, Richard. *The End of All Things Is at Hand.* Bridge-Logos Publishers, 2009.

Other Resources That Were Consulted in the Preparation of This Chapter

1. *Bible Code*. http://2012wiki.com/index.php?title=Bible_Code

Additional Resources You May Wish to Explore

1. The Bible Code, transcript of a story that was broadcast on *BBC Two* on Thursday, November 20, 2003.

15

Do Not Fear!

*What we need right now is courage—the courage to face
the future, with all its glorious potential and all its terrible
possibilities. The price of facing danger is fear, which of course
can be quite unpleasant, even paralyzing at times.
We must demand courage of our leaders, but they will
respond only if we show it ourselves. The mere act of
preparing for the coming tumult will save us, perhaps
physically, and certainly spiritually.*[1]

LAWRENCE E. JOSEPH

Now That We Know, What Do We Do?

As I conclude this writing, I am concerned that I might be
seen as a prophet of doom. I hope that does not happen, for
my purpose in writing this book is to impart information to
you, so that you can draw your own conclusions about the
future and find the hope you need, no matter what the future
holds. I also want to help you prepare, at least spiritually, for
what might happen in the not-too-distant future.

The bulk of this book has been presented in an objective
manner, as I've explored the various viewpoints of so many
different cultures, religions, and individuals. I hope you have
found the information to be interesting and enlightening. Now
I am shifting gears, so to speak, and in this chapter I want to
let you know what I personally believe about these important
matters.

First, let me assure you that I do not believe that we can be at all specific about the date of the end of all things. The fact that the Mayan calendar appears to end on December 21, 2012, does not mean that the world will end on that day, even though there is some evidence from various quarters that tends to support this view.

I am a Christian—a follower of Christ—and, as such, I lean heavily on what the Bible tells us about the end times. Indeed, the Bible is a prophetic book, and it has a great deal to say concerning this topic. Regrettably, I've been able to cover only a small portion of the prophecies one can readily find throughout the Scriptures. I hope you will spend time carefully studying the prophecies of the Bible. This will help you get ready for the things that are to come.

I place the highest value on the words of Jesus and His prophecies about the last days, for He is my Lord and Savior. If you do not know Him personally, the first step to take in preparing for the future is to invite Him into your heart and life.

A Glorious Invitation

The Book of the Revelation is a very prophetic book, but it is also a very personal book, so personal, in fact, that Jesus uses it to extend a glorious invitation to you. He says, *"Here I am! I stand at the door and knock. If anyone hears my voice and opens the door, I will come in and eat with him, and he with me"* (Revelation 3:20, NIV).

He is referring to the door of your heart. Do you sense that He is knocking on your heart-door today? If so, I encourage you to open the door and let Him come in.

The Bible says, *"Yet to all who received him [Jesus], to those who believed in his name, he gave the right to become the children of God"* (John 1:12, NIV). This is another glorious invitation—to become a member of the family of God. Isn't it exciting to know that God, the Father, wants to adopt you as His own child?

Jesus wants you to be born again. He said, *"I tell you the truth, no one can see the kingdom of God unless he is born again"* (John 3:3, NIV). He is referring to the New Birth, and this is something you can experience by believing in Jesus and trusting that He has been resurrected from the dead. Through the New Birth you commit your life to Him. This will require you to repent of your sins and to determine to follow Him, no matter what the cost.

John writes, *"For God so loved the world [you] that he gave his one and only Son, that whoever believes in him shall not perish but have eternal life"* (John 3:16, NIV). Do you know that God loves you? Do you believe in Jesus Christ?

Each person who has ever lived has fallen short of the glory of God, because we are all sinners, as Paul points out, *"For all have sinned and fall short of the glory of God"* (Romans 3:23, NIV). The Great Apostle goes on to say, *"For the wages of sin is death, but the gift of God is eternal life in Christ Jesus our Lord"* (Romans 6:23, NIV).

Do you see how this promise ties in with the central subject of this book? When you know Jesus, you do not have to fear the future, for you are assured of eternal life in Him. This makes all the difference in the world. Indeed, it changes everything, as Paul tells us, *"Therefore, if anyone is in Christ, he is a new creation; the old has gone, the new has come!"* (2 Corinthians 5:17, NIV).

When you repent of your sins and give your life to Christ, everything in your life becomes fresh and new. This does not mean that you won't have problems, but it does mean that you will have divine help to enable you to face whatever may come your way.

If you want to become a child of God, a member of His family, a person who will live forever, and a new creation, please pray as follows: "Heavenly Father, I thank you for sending Jesus to die for me so that I would not perish, but have everlasting life. I repent of my sins, and this means that I am sorry for every sin I've ever committed and I am determining in my heart to walk away from every sin and bad habit in my life. Lord God, I am committing my life to following you and your ways. Please forgive me of my sins. Come into my heart, Lord Jesus. As I reach up and take Your mighty hand, a sense of great peace, forgiveness, and joy floods over my soul. Thank you for giving me newness of life. Thank you for saving me and making me whole. From now on you will have first place in my life."

Welcome to the family of God! You are now free from the guilt of your past, and you are free from all fear of the future. I am sure, therefore, that you can now understand that the commitment you've just made is the first step toward getting ready for the end times.

I hope you will write to me and let me know what this means to you. I will be praying for you, as you endeavor to walk according to God's Word—the holy Bible. I rejoice with you.

PRACTICAL STEPS TO TAKE

I am not a survivalist by any means. However, I do recognize that there are some practical steps to take in order to prepare for and go through hard times, whatever they may be.

1. Reevaluate your priorities. Jesus said, *"But seek first his [God's] kingdom and his righteousness, and all these things will be given to you as well. Therefore do not worry about tomorrow, for tomorrow will worry about itself. Each day has enough trouble of its own"* (Matthew 6:33-34, NIV). What takes first place in your life? These verses command us not to worry about the future. The truth is that worry is a sin in that it blocks our personal relationship with Jesus Christ. In effect, Jesus is saying that we should capture and practice each

present moment of our lives. This reminds me of something Saint Francis said in response to the question, "What would you do if you knew Jesus was coming back today?" He said, "I'd just keep hoeing my garden."

2. Keep good stocks of food and water on hand in the event of a natural disaster.

3. Simplify your life. This might involve downsizing at all levels. This could mean that you should relocate, get rid of things you don't use, and begin saving your money.

4. Gardening and canning. Growing a garden is a wonderfully therapeutic activity that can be enjoyed by the entire family. The harvest you reap from what you sow can be canned or frozen for future consumption, and it is a money saver, as well.

5. Stay healthy. This involves getting good exercise, eating nutritional foods, drinking plenty of water, and other healthful practices. One model I learned long ago is based on the acronym NEWSTART, as shown below:

N—Nutrition
E—Exercise
W—Water
S—Sunlight
T—Temperance
A—Air (Getting plenty of fresh air)
R—Rest
T—Trust

Let's focus on that last word for a minute. The word "trust," from my point of view, is closely related to the word "rest." It is an important biblical concept, as this verse from Proverbs shows: *Trust in the Lord with all your heart and lean not on your own understanding. In all your ways acknowledge him, and he will make your paths straight"* (Proverbs 3:5-6, NIV).

SPIRITUAL STEPS TO TAKE

As a Christian believer, what can you do to prepare personally for the end and to help others prepare along with you? The Bible provides us with several answers to this question:

• **Pray.** In many of His prophecies about the end times Jesus told us to watch and pray. The apostles tell us to do the same. Paul writes, *"Be joyful always; pray continually; give thanks in all circumstances, for this is God's will for you in Christ Jesus"* (1 Thessalonians 5:16-18, NIV). Seldom does the Bible state so specifically and emphatically that something is God's will for us. This passage, though, is clear in saying that we must always pray and always give thanks.

• **Preach.** One of our most important jobs as believers is to lead others to a saving knowledge of Jesus Christ. Knowing that the end of all things is at hand compels us to share the gospel with others. It is true that every person is either a missionary or a mission field. It is also true that every person needs to know Jesus. Therefore, *"Preach the Word; be prepared in season and out of season; correct, rebuke and encourage—with great patience and careful instruction"* (2 Timothy 4:2, NIV).

• **Love.** We are commanded to love God and to love others. This is the mark of a true Christian. The Apostle John writes, *"God is love. Whoever lives in love lives in God, and God in him. In this way, love is made complete among us so that we will have confidence on the day of judgment, because in this world we are like him. There is no fear in love. But perfect love drives out fear, because fear has to do with punishment. The one who fears is not made perfect in love."* (1 John 4:16-18, NIV)

• **Seek a close relationship with the Lord.** He wants to know you in a personal and intimate way. The better you know Him, the better your life will be. This is a guarantee I can make without any qualifications.

What is the worst thing that can happen to you? Is it death? As someone has said, we are all terminally ill. It is just a matter of time. As a believer, you know that death is not the end; it is actually a whole new beginning.

The manner of our death is less important than how we face death. Does it make much difference in the light of eternity if we die as a result of some cataclysmic disaster, such as those that have been predicted by so many, or from old age or some disease?

Let us face the future with the confidence that comes from faith and trust. Jesus said, *"Peace I leave with you; my peace I give you. I do not give to you as the world gives. Do not let your hearts be troubled and do not be afraid"* (John 14:27, NIV).

This supernatural peace is available to you now. Therefore, *"Do not be anxious about anything, but in everything, by prayer and petition, with thanksgiving, present your requests to God. And the peace of God, which transcends all understanding, will guard your hearts and your minds in Christ Jesus"* (Philippians 4:6-7, NIV).

"Never be afraid to trust an unknown future to a known God" (Corrie ten Boom).

Endnotes

1. Joseph, Lawrence E. *Apocalypse 2012*. Broadway Books, New York, 2007.

INDEX

Votan, Pacal vii, 1, 9, 10, 13, 15, 17, 21

W

Waller, Joanne 100
Web Bot Project vii, 221, 222, 223, 224, 225, 226
Wheel of Time 84, 175
White Feather 73
Whitehead, Alfred North 57
Wilkerson, Rev. David 102
Wilson, Robert Anton 59
Winter Solstice of 2012 5
World Trade Center 106, 218, 223
World War III 71, 72, 82, 108, 125, 168
Wyllt, Myrddin 95

Y

yang 55
Year of Transformation 224
Yellowstone National Park 97, 230
yin 55
Young, Rev. David 72
Yucatan Peninsula 3

Z

Zapotec 47
Zero state 53, 55, 56
Zodiac 7
Zohar 194
Zoroaster 180, 181, 182, 187
Zoroastrians vii, x, 163, 180, 181, 182